D1244198

Equestrian

TITLES IN THIS SERIES INCLUDE:

SCIENCE BEHIND SPORTS

Equestrian

TONEY ALLMAN

LUCENT BOOKS
A part of Gale, Cengage Learning

GALE
CENGAGE Learning·

Detroit • New York • San Francisco • New Haven, Conn • Waterville, Maine • London

© 2014 Gale, Cengage Learning

Every effort has been made to trace the owners of copyrighted material.

LIBRARY OF CONGRESS CATALOGING-IN-PUBLICATION DATA

Allman, Toney.
  Equestrian / by Toney Allman.
      pages cm. -- (Science behind sports)
  Includes bibliographical references and index.
  ISBN 978-1-4205-1138-3 (hardcover)
  1. Horsemanship--Juvenile literature. 2. Horsemanship--Physiological aspects.
  3. Sports sciences--Juvenile literature. I. Title.
  SF309.2.A55 2014
  688.7'6--dc23
                              2013035700

Lucent Books
27500 Drake Rd
Farmington Hills MI 48331

ISBN-13: 978-1-4205-1138-3
ISBN-10: 1-4205-1138-6

Printed in the United States of America
1 2 3 4 5 6 7 17 16 15 14 13

CONTENTS

FOREWORD

O n March 21, 1970, Slovenian ski jumper Vinko Bogataj took a terrible fall while competing at the Ski-Flying World Championships in Oberstdorf, West Germany. Bogataj's pinwheeling crash was caught on tape by an ABC *Wide World of Sports* film crew and eventually became synonymous with "the agony of defeat" in competitive sporting. While many viewers were transfixed by the severity of Bogataj's accident, most were not aware of the biomechanical and environmental elements behind the skier's fall—heavy snow and wind conditions that made the ramp too fast and Bogataj's inability to maintain his center of gravity and slow himself down. Bogataj's accident illustrates that, no matter how mentally and physically prepared an athlete may be, scientific principles—such as momentum, gravity, friction, and aerodynamics—always have an impact on performance.

Lucent Books' Science Behind Sports series explores these and many more scientific principles behind some of the most popular team and individual sports, including baseball, hockey, gymnastics, wrestling, swimming, and skiing. Each volume in the series focuses on one sport or group of related sports. The volumes open with a brief look at the featured sport's origins, history and changes, then move on to cover the biomechanics and physiology of playing, related health and medical concerns, and the causes and treatment of sports-related injuries.

In addition to learning about the arc behind a curve ball, the impact of centripetal force on a figure skater, or how water buoyancy helps swimmers, Science Behind Sports readers will also learn how exercise, training, warming up, and diet and nutrition directly relate to peak performance and enjoyment of the sport. Volumes may also cover why certain sports are popular, how sports function in the business world, and which hot sporting issues—sports doping and cheating, for example—are in the news.

Basic physical science concepts, such as acceleration, kinetics, torque, and velocity, are explained in an engaging and accessible manner. The full-color text is augmented by fact boxes, sidebars, photos, and detailed diagrams, charts and graphs. In addition, a subject-specific glossary, bibliography and index provide further tools for researching the sports and concepts discussed throughout Science Behind Sports.

CHAPTER 1

An Overview of Equestrian Competitive Sports

Competitions among horses and riders have been in existence almost since the time humans began using horses for practical purposes, such as to help with agricultural work or hunting. Historians say that the first competitions were likely races in which prehistoric humans competed to see whose horse was fastest and which rider was the most skilled. For thousands of years, horse competitions such as these were informal, but in modern times, formal sporting events with standards, rules, and rankings have become popular all over the world. These events involve myriad equestrian competitions, or disciplines, from horse racing to endurance competitions to organized games. No matter what the equestrian sport, the human half of the athletic partnership has the best chance of success when he or she has an understanding of the scientific principles involved in horse movement and horsemanship. Even for a skill as simple as balancing on the back of a horse and not falling off there is a scientific explanation.

The Horse and Human Partnership

The partnership between humans and horses dates back thousands of years. Horses were originally hunted for food by Stone Age peoples of prehistory, which lasted some

2.5 million years until about 8000 B.C. However, archae-ologists say that horses were domesticated for human use on the Eurasian steppes, in an area of the world that now includes western Kazakhstan, Ukraine, and southwest Russia. Domesticating an animal is not the same as taming an animal. A horse taken from the wild when very young and raised with humans may be tame; it is adapted to living with people and can be taught to obey its owner. However, that horse is still a wild animal. William J. Jordan, a British veterinarian, explains, "Domestication is a process whereby man has structurally, physiologically and behaviourally modified certain species of animals by maintaining them in or near human habitation and by breeding from those certain animals who seem best suited for various human objectives."[1]

A man rears his horse in the Kyrgyzstan countryside. It is believed that horses were first domesticated in the vast steppes of this part of the world.

Although they could not understand the science behind domesticating horses, the first domesticators could choose to breed captured, tame horses that had the characteristics that were most desirable. They could mate the friendliest, calmest horses together in the hope that friendlier offspring

TROT & GALLOP

No one knows why, but the shins, or cannon bones, of domesticated horses are thinner than the shins of wild horses. This fact helps scientists studying ancient horse skeletons to date the period when horses were domesticated.

would be born. They could breed together those horses that had longer legs or bigger bodies or that were the most willing to carry riders on their backs. In this way, over time and generations, the horses that best met human needs were selected, and different breeds of horses developed. On the Eurasian steppes, docile, calm temperaments were perhaps considered desirable traits. Archaeologists have found evidence that these first domesticated horses were milked and wore bridles, probably for riding and maybe for being led while carrying loads.

The earliest breeds of domesticated horses proved so valuable to humans that their use spread rapidly throughout Europe and Asia and eventually throughout the world. Horses, more than any other animal, had a profound effect on human civilization. British archaeologist Alan Outram says, "One thing that is clear is that the domestic horse revolutionized human life, making us much more mobile, changing our trade patterns and modes of warfare. Such changes affected the whole way in which societies were organized and interacted with each other."[2] People used horses for transportation, to carry trade goods across long distances, as muscle power for work such as lifting or dragging and pulling, and in warfare. As uses became more varied, breeds suited to different activities were slowly developed. Whether pulling war chariots for ancient Chinese or Roman armies, carrying military cavalries into battle, herding livestock in the American West, or elegantly pulling a rich man's carriage, horses became important and necessary partners in many human endeavors.

The History of Organized Horse Sports

Whatever the need for horses was in daily life, sports competitions were a natural outcome of their practical use. The ancient Greeks, Romans, and Byzantines, for example, held chariot race competitions. The horse-drawn chariot was the most important battlefield technological invention of its time. Pulled by teams of two to four swift, powerful horses, chariots carried warriors into battle and helped ancient conquerors establish empires. By as early as 1300 B.C., evidence of chariot races appears in ancient Greece, and chariot racing was an extremely popular event in the early Olympic Games. In ancient Rome, chariot racing at the Circus Maximus arena drew crowds of people numbering two hundred thousand. The drivers in chariot racing were initially gladiators and warriors, but later professional drivers were the sports stars of their day. They drove super-light chariots that were totally unsuitable for war and were built only for the sport. The horses, too, were athletes, bred exclusively for racing. Chariot racing required not just speed,

A second century A.D. mosaic depicts equestrian sporting events inside an arena.

but also endurance and courage from horse and driver, and skill in balancing the lightweight chariot, coping with the difficulties of making sharp turns on the track, avoiding falls for both horse and charioteer, and dealing with collisions with the wall or other chariots.

In both Greece and Rome, mounted horse racing was also a competition event, along with chariot racing. Horse and rider were a competitive partnership, and spectators bet on their favorite horses. When the Roman Empire fell in A.D. 476, spectacular sporting events declined, but in other parts of the world, such as Persia and Turkey, horsemen played games such as polo as training for cavalries going into battle. By the twelfth century A.D., English knights returned home from fighting in the Crusades with captured Arab horses, and horse racing was on its way to becoming "the sport of kings." Only the wealthy nobility could afford to own these racehorses, and by breeding them with English horses, the owners developed the first Thoroughbred animals—known for being swift, strong, and agile. In modern professional sporting events—which began in England in the eighteenth century—Thoroughbred racing was a test of skills including endurance, speed, balance (for both horse and rider), agility, and courage. These horses were bred for sport and pleasure—not war or other practical use—and competition for competition's sake became extremely popular. As time passed, other equestrian sports became popular, and each tested skills of the horse and rider that may have originated in practical uses but became sports in their own right. Dressage, for example, is a sport in which the art of riding in tune with the horse's graceful natural movements is tested. It began with the art of training horse and rider for cavalry movements on the battlefield, but it has become a test of the horse-and-rider team's ability to cooperate with each other with precision and beauty.

Throughout most of the horse's sports history, people did not really understand the scientific principles involved in the skills required in equestrian sports. Even when the science behind the sport was not obvious, however, humans tried to determine and breed for the strongest, fittest, fastest, most able horse for which the animal was needed. They

"Leader of Ten Thousand"

In Mongolia, sturdy Mongolian horses have been trea-sured and depended on for centuries, and today, even among city dwellers, these horses are still loved and valued. Every July, the most important festival for Mongolians—the Naadam Festival—includes horse racing. The races occur on the open plains, and the riders are boys between five and twelve years old. The biggest, most important race is held about 30 miles (48.3km) outside the Mongolian capi-tal of Ulan Bator. In a race 17 miles (27.4km) long, horses and riders tear across the steppes, competing both for prize money and prestige. Some of the horses belong to well-off city owners of hundreds of horses; many belong to nomadic tribespeople who bring one or two horses for the race. The boy jockeys often ride bareback (without a saddle) and wear only socks on their feet because they think shoes might hurt the horses. Many sing songs of encouragement to their horses during the race. The first five horses to complete the race are honored. The riders drink mare's milk and sprinkle some on the horses' backs. The boy who wins the race is dubbed "leader of ten thousand" and wins the money, but it is the horse that receives the medal.

recognized the superior ability of the skilled horseman in comparison to the average rider, but they could not ex-plain the skill in scientific terms. Today, that situation has changed; the science behind equestrian sports is carefully researched and studied so that the horse and human team can perform to its optimal ability.

Modern Non-Jumping Sports

Organized competitions with horses are many and varied, but the skills required and the science involved are often essentially the same. Equestrian competitions can be orga-nized into jumping and non-jumping sports. Non-jumping

USING HORSES FOR WORK AND PLAY

The 2009–2010 Equine Industry Study, conducted by American Horse Publications, found that among the almost 11,000 respondents to their survey, pleasure and trail riding were the most common uses for horses, at 73.5 percent. Dressage came in second with 26.3 percent, while sports such as racing, polo, and rodeo came in at less than 5 percent.

How do you use your horses?

Activity	Percent
Barrel racing	10.2%
Breeding	19.8%
Breed shows	17.8%
Cutting	3.2%
Dressage	26.3%
Driving	9.6%
Endurance	5.2%
Fox hunting	5.3%
Hunters	12.9%
Jumpers	10.6%
Lessons/Training	25.1%
Natural Horsemanship	22.7%
Pleasure/Trail Riding	73.5%
Polo	0.5%
Racing	2.6%
Reining	7.2%
Rodeo	4.5%
Roping	4.9%
Saddleseat	2.6%
Steeplechasing	0.3%
Team Penning	5.1%
Working	11.6%
None of these	1.5%
Other	16.5%

Source: 2009–2010 American Horse Publications Equine Industry Survey. American Horse Publications. www.americanhorsepubs.org/resources /AHP-Equine-Survey-Final.pdf.

sports include such competitions as mounted games, dressage, endurance events, Western riding, and racing. Polo, for example, is a mounted game. At its highest level, it is an international professional sport in which two opposing teams of four players each compete to hit a polo ball using long mallets down a 300-yard field (274.3m) and through goalposts. The teams of mounted competitors ride highly trained polo ponies and are skilled horsemen and women who can maintain control of themselves and their horses as they race up and down the field, make agile turns, and perform quick stops and starts. New Zealand professional polo player Mark Harris says, "You've got half-tonne animals running at 25 to 30 mph trying to hit a little white ball. It's fast and glamorous, but the glamour wears off the more you're around polo. You soon realise it's hard work, and time consuming."[3] Harris explains that a polo player's success begins with the conformation, or physical structure, of the horse, because the horse's conformation determines its physical ability in the game. The horse's temperament matters, too, so Harris always prefers a horse that is calm as well as strong and fast. The human half of the equation must be skillful, also, with the balance, strength, and co-ordination to control the horse and cope with the natural forces of gravity and physics that affect the movements of both horse and rider and put them at risk of missteps, falls, missed shots, and injury.

The skills and abilities required for polo are also evident in Western riding events. Western riding, which includes rodeo-style events, is a sport developed in the American West and based on the skills needed for hunting, herding, and riding the ranges. It is a test of how comfortable a horse is for the seated rider, how well the horse and rider perform reining exercises, and how agile both are when quickly cutting an animal out of a herd or racing around a series of barrels or poles. As with polo, the Western horse must be not only fast, but trained and bred to be calm and cooperative. Balancing skills for both horse and rider are also imperative. In any competitive equestrian event, the rider or handler has to maintain his or her balance. When the horse moves forward, the unprepared human is moved backward.

When the horse halts, the unbalanced human is propelled forward. Given the quick starts and sharp turns, balance for both horse and rider means functioning despite the natural forces, such as a changing center of gravity, that can lead to failure or falls.

In competitive horse racing, a calm horse may not be the best horse. Balance and speed, along with the energy needed to overcome natural forces such as gravity, are paramount. Thoroughbred horses are built for speed, and Thoroughbred horse racing is a professional sport worldwide. The horses have pedigrees—charts or tables that list their parentage, relations, and ancestry—and are registered with professional associations to guarantee their lineage. They have been bred for their conformation, energy, stamina, speed, and racing spirit. Professional jockeys, who ride the horses during a race, are as much athletes as their Thoroughbred mounts. Jockeys are usually small in stature and weight, but they are strong and courageous, with balancing skills, the ability to control a high-spirited animal, good coordination, and quick reflexes. All of these abilities are necessary to ensure that the horse can gallop at top speed to the finish line, avoid stumbling or bumping into another horse, and maintain enough energy to complete the race in a winning time. In other kinds of horse races, such as quarter horse racing or harness racing (in which the horse pulls the handler in a light two-wheeled cart at a fast trot instead of a gallop), similar skills are required.

Dressage is a different kind of non-jumping sport in which balance and spirit are required but speed is not. At the top level of competition—the Olympic dressage events—horse and rider are a highly trained team. Training the horse to perform precise movements on command is the goal of the handler, and these movements demand strength from the horse, as well as calmness and responsiveness. Both horse and rider must appear to be in balance with each other, and the horse must be able to recognize and respond to the slightest

TROT & GALLOP

Equestrian events are the only competitions at the Olympic Games in which men and women compete against each other.

Adelinde Cornelissen of the Netherlands and Parzival compete in the individual dressage event at the 2012 Summer Olympics in London, England.

movements and pressures of the rider's body. Training for the horse involves strengthening muscles, developing body language and communication skills, as well as being taught particular movements and even learning to stand immobile. When performed correctly, dressage is an elegant sport that also requires a significant amount of muscular endurance on the part of both horse and rider.

Endurance riding is a non-jumping sport requiring a different kind of endurance than dressage. Endurance riding is long-distance racing that may cover up to 100 miles (160km). It is a test of the stamina of both horse and rider as well as speed—not the sprinting speed of the Thoroughbred horse race, but staying power and endurance. Endurance riding is also a test of human intelligence and control; the rider must pace the horse, riding at different speeds depending upon conditions so as to ensure that the horse does not lose the energy to finish the race. The sciences relating to motion and energy, physical body structure and psychological behavior, and the fitness and conditioning of human and animal bodies are all behind one's success in non-jumping equestrian sports.

Modern Jumping Sports

Jumping sports include show jumping, hunting, and some racing and cross-country endurance events. The scientific principles and laws that influence these sports can include all of those that affect non-jumping sports, but with the added complication of leaping over obstacles. Equestrian experts Judith Draper, Debby Sly, and Sarah Muir say, "Jumping needs confidence, rhythm and balance."[4] In hunting and cross-country events, the obstacles are natural ones, such as ditches, watercourses, farmer's fencing, fallen trees, and brush. In some racing events, the obstacles may be human-made and include jumping a fence and landing in a water obstacle on the other side. Racing competitions such as steeplechase may include jumping a series of fences in a row or jumping obstacles that are soft brush (or plastic imitations) and then those that are solid, such as timber fences. Show jumping is an Olympic equestrian sport that takes place on a course of artificial jumps instead of natural cross-country obstacles. At the sport's highest level, it is called Grand Prix show jumping and includes obstacles of varying heights and difficulty. These obstacles may include different kinds of fences, stacked bars, water obstacles, and simulated stone walls. At the Olympic level of competition, obstacles may be more than 5 feet (1.5m) in height and up to 6 feet (1.8m) wide. At times, neither the horse nor the rider is able to see the landing area on the other side.

Whatever the jumping sport, extreme physical effort is required for both the horse and the rider. Courage, strength, balance, and fitness are needed, but extra bursts of energy are also needed to gain the momentum to clear each jump. Overcoming the force of gravity to launch oneself into the air simply requires more force and energy than trotting or galloping. For the rider, just staying on the jumping horse's back can be difficult. Horses ridden in jumping sports have to be trained and conditioned to jump higher and higher and to increase their speed as they take the jumps, while riders must train to develop muscle strength and agility. Says horse expert Heather Toms, "The best show jumpers

Patrick Nisbett competes in the individual jump event at the 2010 World Equestrian Games in Lexington, Kentucky.

A Famous Designer

Pamela Carruthers was an internationally famous designer of Grand Prix show jumping courses. She was born in Scotland in 1916 and competed as a show jumper during the 1940s. Then, for thirty years, she specialized in designing courses for jumping competitions. Designing jumps and laying out the courses required that she be a creative artist and landscaper and make the course beautiful and original. Carruthers also had to have the skills to ensure that the jumps would stand up to the competition and test the abilities of horse and rider. She needed to understand how to lay out a series of different kinds of obstacles that made the whole course difficult but not impossible. Carruthers is best known for her innovative design of oxers—obstacles with two rails set side by side to make the jump wider or a brush jump with a rail set in front, at the takeoff side. Carruthers designed courses where only a few competitors could clear the first round without making mistakes.

Carruthers died in 2003, but her influence continues today as modern designers follow her example in creating Grand Prix courses.

are accurate and courageous; they need to be brave enough to attempt tall obstacles and physically tough enough to go through the most demanding of courses. Obviously, the most talented horses also need to be ridden by the most talented riders."[5]

To Enjoy the Sport, Know the Science

In all equestrian sports, talent and an understanding of how to develop that talent are necessary for success, whether the horse-and-rider team is jumping, racing, or showing off their ability to work together. The body of information and ideas garnered over the centuries of human/horse partnership has combined to produce the best horses and the best riders for each individual sport. Knowledge of the science behind these sports can only increase the delight and fascination that people have for equestrian competitions by increasing their appreciation for the skills and abilities of both the horses and the humans who guide them.

CHAPTER **2**

The Physics of Equestrian Sports

P hysics is the science that deals with matter and energy and how they interact with each other. Matter can be in any form or size, from the particles that make up an atom to a drop of water to a muscle to a whole body or even a star. Energy can be found in a number of forms, including motion, light, electricity, and chemical reactions. When relating physics to equestrian sports, however, the matter is the horse or the rider, and the energy is primarily in the form of motion. The physics of motion is about forces, particularly the forces that can act on a body that initiate motion or cause changes in motion. The rules, or laws, that explain motion, especially with sports involving racing or jumping, are the basic laws of physics, which can help explain the performance of both the horse and the handler.

Types of Motion

In a Thoroughbred horse race, a swift, powerful animal carrying a professional jockey must make a fast start from a standing position, reach a galloping speed, and maintain that speed—hopefully, faster than any other horse—in order to cross the finish line first and win the race. In the seventeenth century, a physicist named Sir Isaac Newton proposed three basic laws of physics that can be applied to equestrian events like this one. These laws explain the motion of the horse and the forces that it must utilize or overcome to start and finish the race.

Newton's laws describe specific types of motion and changes in motion using scientifically defined terms and simple mathematical equations. Speed, for example, is a measure of the distance traveled in a certain amount of time. Velocity is a physics concept that is related to speed, but speed and velocity are not exactly the same. Speed is a measure of the change in distance over time, while velocity is a measure of how far in a certain direction an object (like a racehorse) moves as the result of an applied force. Velocity describes both speed and direction.

To achieve a change in velocity, a body (like the horse at the starting gate) must accelerate. Acceleration is defined as the amount of time needed to achieve that change in velocity. The smaller the acceleration time, the faster a body reaches a change in velocity. (In physics, acceleration refers simply to a change in velocity over time. Acceleration, in this sense, can mean either speeding up or slowing down.) Both acceleration and velocity are related to another important physics concept at play during equestrian sports: momentum. Momentum (abbreviated as mV) is a measure of the amount of motion a body has. The amount of momentum a horse has depends on two things—its mass (how much of it there is) and its velocity. Physicists express this relationship in a simple formula: Momentum equals mass times velocity. As the horse is racing down the track, it has momentum, and that momentum is directly related to how quickly it can cross the finish line. Momentum, as well as the concepts of

Weight or Mass?

Scientists are careful to distinguish between the definitions of weight and mass. Mass is a quantity; a measurement of the amount of matter that is in an object. Weight is a measure of how strongly the force of gravity is pulling on the object. Mass does not change in a human or a horse, but since weight depends on gravity, it can change when an object leaves the earth. For example, an object on the moon weighs less than the same object would on earth because the moon has less gravity than earth does. Practically, if an object stays on the earth, where gravity is always the same, there is no difference between weight and mass. In physics, however, weight and mass are related to each other but are measures of two different amounts.

Horses stand waiting at the starting gate for a 2008 race in Melbourne, Australia.

mass, velocity, and acceleration, are important in understanding Newton's laws of motion and how they relate to a horse's performance.

Inertia at the Starting Gate

The first of Newton's three laws is the law of inertia. It states: "Every object persists in its state of rest or uniform motion in a straight line unless it is compelled to change that state by forces impressed on it."[6] At the starting gate, the horse is the object at a state of rest at the beginning of the race. The animal overcomes inertia by applying force with its framework of skeleton and muscles to propel it forward.

A force is any push or pull on an object as the result of its interaction with another object. It is anything that changes the state of motion of an object. In the case of the racehorse at the starting gate, the force is the horse's push against the ground with its hooves in order to accelerate. The amount of force required to change the horse's veloc-

When gates open, racehorses quickly go from being still to moving at high velocity.

ity from standing still to moving is explained by Newton's second law.

A Fast Start and Newton's Second Law

Newton's second law says: "Force is equal to the change in momentum (mV) per change in time. For a constant mass, force equals mass times acceleration."[7] This law is really a mathematical formula: F (force) = m (mass) × a (acceleration). The horse's body is the constant mass in this law (its size does not change during a race). The force that the horse applies with its muscles results in the change in its velocity, and the amount of force applied directly influences the horse's acceleration. The greater the force applied to the mass, the greater the acceleration. This formula is one way of understanding horses' speed during a racing event. Newton's second law shows that as force is applied, an object accelerates (changes its velocity), and the velocity is in the same direction as the force. A winning horse accelerates and changes its velocity

A DANGEROUS SPORT FOR HORSES?

Horses face grave risks while racing. In 2011 there were 1.88 fatal injuries recorded for every 1,000 race starts, with the most injuries occurring with older horses, on dirt tracks, and in shorter races.

Racing-Related Equine Fatalities in 2012

	Starts	Fatalities per 1,000 Starts
Age		
2	27,316	1.39
3	108,545	1.85
4+	233,704	2.01
Surface		
Turf	53,991	1.74
Dirt	271,851	2.10
Synthetic	43,723	1.03
Distance		
<6F	88,536	2.35
6F–8F	214,525	1.78
>8F	66,504	1.80

Note: 1F (furlong) = 220 yards

Source: The Jockey Club. Equine injury database statistics. www.jockeyclub.com/pdfs/supplemental tables_eid.pdf.

faster than the other horses on the track, moving in the same direction. The faster horse goes farther in a shorter distance of time than the slower horses, and will win the race.

Horse racing experts say that a horse's ability to make a fast break from the starting gate is a critical part of the race. Trainer Holly Robinson explains, "So many races are won or lost in the starting gate. If a horse gets a slow start from the gate, stumbles, or has a bad break it is nearly impossible to make up for it when all the others broke well."[8] Newton's first two laws are applicable to the fast break in terms of the force applied by the horse and its velocity and acceleration. The third law is demonstrated in the fast break, too, but it is most obvious when something goes wrong.

Pushing Forward: Newton's Third Law

Newton's third law states: "For every action, there is an equal and opposite re-action."[9] This means that when a horse exerts a force on the ground with its hooves, the ground pushes back with the same amount of force. Of course, this force does not cause the earth to move—its size is vastly greater than the horse's size—but the earth does push back. Physics professor Donald Simanek explains, "The horse places its feet so as to change the angle of the force its hooves exert on the ground, thereby increasing the backward force of its hooves on the ground. The backward reaction force of the ground on the horse's hooves therefore increases, by Newton's third law. . . . What force pushes the horse forward? It's the force exerted by the ground! The horse pushes backward on the ground, so the ground pushes forward with an equal force. If the horse pushes back against the ground . . . the horse will accelerate."[10]

Newton's third law applies to all aspects of the horse's performance. The horse gallops toward the finish line with hooves pushing against the earth with as much force as its muscles can provide. The more force that is applied, the greater the hoof-push and the greater the push back from the earth and the more the horse accelerates. Sometimes, however, the angle at which a horse pushes with its hoof may

TROT & GALLOP

To make money after his 1935 Olympic gold medal wins, famous runner Jesse Owens staged short races against horses. Owens usually won, but only because he got the official starter to fire the starting pistol close to the competing horse's ear, making the horse startle and rear and giving Owens a head start.

be askew, perhaps because the horse placed its foot wrong or because its hoof happened to strike a bump or depression in the ground. If that happens, the horse may stumble because the ground pushed back but in an exactly equal and opposite direction—the direction of the wrong angle. A different kind of mishap may occur in sand or wet mud. The horse may slide like a car does on an icy road. The horse cannot push hard enough on the ground because it gives instead of resisting the push, so the ground does not push back enough to enable the horse to propel forward. The mud is not fixed in place the way solid ground is, and the horse sinks or skids.

The Jockey and Newton's Laws

In a horse race, the jockey is as subject to Newton's laws as the horse. When a horse propels forward at the starting gate, its jockey tends to be thrown backward. This is a result of Newton's first law. When both horse and rider

Horses and their riders approach the finish line at a 2012 race. Both inertia and momentum have important effects on the jockey.

are at rest, they remain at rest. Both are subject to inertia. When the horse moves forward, the lower part of the jockey's body, which is in contact with the horse's body, moves forward, too. The upper part of the jockey's body, however, is not in contact and tends to remain at rest. Because of inertia, the jockey who is unprepared seems to lean backward. Professional jockeys, aware of this phenomenon, adjust quickly by using their own internal muscular forces to lean forward with the horse. Even the best jockey, however, can be subject to the forces of the first law if a horse stops suddenly as it is galloping along the racecourse. The stop may be due to a sudden injury to a leg, a bump into another object, or a mistake that causes the horse to stumble and fall. If the horse's forward momentum is interrupted, the jockey continues moving forward as Newton's first law predicts. Inertia means that a body in motion tends to remain in motion unless acted on by a force—that is, unless something stops it. The jockey flies forward unless his or her momentum is interrupted.

In a serious accident on the racecourse, the jockey can fly forward, off the horse, until he or she hits the ground because of gravity. Gravity is the attraction between any objects that have mass. Its strength depends on the distance of the objects from each other and the amount of mass that they have. Close objects have a greater attractive force toward each other than distant objects. Gravity is the outside force that slows the forward motion of the jockey when the horse abruptly stops. The mass of the earth is so large in comparison to the mass of a jockey and the jockey is so close

Death at the Racetrack

In the summer of 2012, professional jockey Jorge Herrera was killed during a racing accident at a track in northern California. Herrera's horse apparently clipped the heels of a horse in front of it with its hooves. Herrera's horse stumbled in mid-gallop, and the jockey was thrown forward, over the horse's head. The horse regained its balance and continued running, but Herrera died of severe head trauma. In the fast speed of the race, no one could see whether a horse stepped on the jockey as he lay on the track. Herrera had suffered racing injuries three times before his fatal accident. According to the manager of the Jockeys' Guild, a trade association representing professional jockeys, jockeys have the most dangerous job in all of sports based on the number of injuries and deaths that they incur. In 2011 almost 20 percent of all Jockeys' Guild members were on temporary disability because of racetrack injuries.

to the earth that gravitational force pulls the jockey to the ground, ending his or her forward motion very quickly. Falling from a galloping horse is more likely to cause serious injury than falling off a walking horse because of the rider's momentum. The greater the momentum, the harder the rider hits the ground. Momentum means "amount of motion" and is defined for a falling jockey just as it is for a galloping horse; it is the jockey's mass times his or her velocity. According to the mathematical formula of Newton's law of universal gravitation (which ties together and expands upon his three laws of motion), momentum and gravity interact to increase the force of impact. It is the momentum, not actually gravity, which causes the injury to the jockey.

Physics and Jumping Sports

The physics laws that describe horse racing are also demonstrated in jumping sports. The process of the horse's jump can be divided into five phases: the approach, takeoff, flight, landing, and recovery. The approach is the distance from which the horse must begin running in order to launch itself from the ground with enough velocity and height to clear an obstacle. A running horse can launch higher than a walking horse because the velocity at the point of its takeoff is greater. Mathematically, physicists have determined that the horse needs to take off from a distance as far away as the jump is high. So a horse trying to jump a 4-foot fence (1.2m) must begin its takeoff 4 feet (1.2m) away from the obstacle. The actual takeoff then follows Newton's laws.

The horse pushes against the ground with its back legs (the force applied to change motion described in Newton's first law); the force has to be enough to accelerate the horse's mass upward and forward (Newton's second law); and the ground pushes back with equal force (Newton's third law).

As the horse's hooves leave the ground after takeoff, the horse's motion then be-

TROT & GALLOP

The average horse gallops at an average speed of 25 to 30 miles (40 to 48km) per hour.

Although it is an enjoyable and entertaining sport, horse racing can also turn deadly. Between 1992 and 2006, there were 79 fatalities among those working with racehorses, including jockeys and groomers.

Horse Racing Deaths, by Occupation, 1992–2006

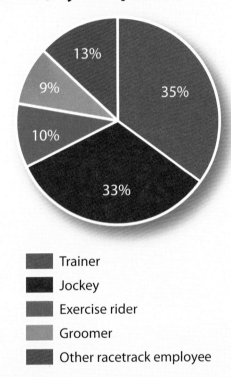

13%
9%
35%
10%
33%

■ Trainer
■ Jockey
■ Exercise rider
■ Groomer
■ Other racetrack employee

Source: Kitty J. Hendricks et al. "An Overview of Safety and Health for Workers in the Horse-Racing Industry." Cincinnati, OH: US Department of Health and Human Services, Centers for Disease Control and Prevention, and National Institute for Occupational Safety and Health, 2009. www.cdc.gov/niosh/docs/2009-128/pdfs/2009-128.pdf.

comes what is known in physics as projectile motion, with the horse as a projectile. A projectile is any object upon which the only force acting is gravity. (The horse is no longer applying any muscular force.) The horse's body is in flight, in a trajectory that becomes an arc or parabola, as its momentum carries it vertically and horizontally while gravity pulls it down.

The horse, thrown upward and forward by the angle at which it pushed to leave the ground, continues its motion by its inertia and returns to the earth only because the outside force of gravity acts upon its flight. Whether the horse clears the fence during its flight phase depends on the velocity it generated at takeoff. One of the most important determinants of a sufficient velocity is the mass of the horse, because horses with greater muscle mass in relation to their body size are able to generate more force. The greater the force, the higher the horse can jump. According to an educational project at the University of North Carolina, a show-jumping horse has enough mass and force that it can launch itself over a fence at a velocity of 26 feet (8m) per second.

The combination of the force of gravity and the horse's momentum determines the success or failure of a horse's landing and recovery. At the time the horse's hooves hit the ground when it lands, the horse's momentum and gravity determine the force of the impact. If the impact is too great,

A photo of Gotta Take Care—being ridden to victory by jockey John Allen in a 2013 hurdle race—illustrates that a horse is a projectile while in mid-jump.

the horse may stumble, fall, or injure itself, but if the jump goes well, the force of landing results in an equal upward force from the ground (Newton's third law) that enables the horse to stop its downward momentum and then recover and start moving toward the next obstacle.

When the Jump Fails

In a jumping event, horse and rider must function as one unit, and both are subject to the same physical forces at the same time. This means that while the horse is in the flight phase of the jump, so is the rider. The flight phase of show jumping can be exhilarating for the rider. For example, since she was a child, show jumper Jennifer Wooten has loved the sport. She explains, "I loved jumping, because there was this exhilarating feeling of freedom when I was flying through the air on my pony. It was just so much fun!"[11] Flying through the air is the easy part of the physics of jumping for the rider. The takeoff and landing phases, however, can be dangerous and difficult. Just as a jockey is thrown backward or forward as a horse propels forward or stops abruptly during a horse race, so is the rider jarred during the takeoff and landing in a show jumping event. If the rider does not use his or her own muscular force to counteract Newton's first law, a fall is inevitable. A fall on landing is especially dangerous because the horse is landing at an angle, aiming downward at the end of its parabolic flight. The angle is generally about forty-five degrees. From that position, a rider will fall head down, risking a serious injury to the head or neck.

Horses and riders are in particular danger if the jump is not cleared successfully. Sometimes a horse will balk—meaning it suddenly stops and refuses to take the jump. The horse's approach momentum, however, determines how quickly it can stop. The greater the momentum, the more force must be applied, and the longer the time it takes to come to a stop. This is explained by Newton's second law (F=ma). The horse stops by applying a force to change its velocity. If the horse's momentum is such that it cannot change its velocity in enough time to stop safely, both horse

A jockey falls from her horse during an attempted jump at the 1985 Badminton Horse Trials in Gloucestershire, England.

and rider may collide with the obstacle. The result can be disastrous. In Ocala, Florida, in 2007, for example, during a cross-country endurance event that included several jumps, a horse named Mr. Barnabus balked at a jump, crashed into the jump obstacle head on, and broke its neck. The horse died instantly, and in its fall, it rolled over onto its rider, twenty-one-year-old Eleanor Brennan. She was crushed by the impact and died.

Jumping horses may also fall because they are unable to clear an obstacle and fall on or over it. When a horse crashes through a fence or other barrier, its momentum is abruptly changed by the force of the collision. Darren Chiacchia, a skilled performer in cross-country eventing, experienced such a collision in 2008. His horse failed to clear the jump, fell, and landed on top of him. Chiacchia almost died from the impact.

Horses and riders in jumping events are involved in dangerous sports. Some people rank all equestrian sports among the most dangerous sports in which people participate. However, the natural physical capability of the horse plays a big part in success and safety. The rider can also influence the outcome. How the rider sits, uses the reins, or uses his or her muscles to coordinate with the horse's efforts affects the ability of the horse to complete any sporting task.

CHAPTER 3

Biomechanics and the Horse and Rider

Biomechanics, says zoologist Steven Vogel, "looks at the technology of life, at the mechanical world of nature."[12] For horses, this means the study of the mechanical systems of the living body, such as how the muscles and tendons move the skeletal system to overcome gravity. In equestrian sports, the biomechanical concepts of energy, efficiency, balance, and power relate to the horse's locomotion, endurance, center of gravity, and ultimately the horse's success in a particular sport. The human handler who understands biomechanics optimizes the performance of the horse-and-rider team.

Horse Locomotion and Gaits

The biomechanics of movement explains a horse's locomotion. Veterinarian Hilary M. Clayton explains, "Locomotion is the act of moving from one location to another. Movement of the entire horse involves independent motion of many body parts, primarily the limbs, but also the trunk, head, and neck. At any moment, different parts of the horse's body may be moving at different speeds and in different directions."[13] The horse's body structure determines how it moves. Its bones are the basic structure of its body; the ligaments (bands of connective tissue) connect the bones together

When horses gallop, all hooves leave the ground. In the late nineteenth century Eadweard Muybridge was the first person to conclusively demonstrate this fact with photographic studies such as this one.

while allowing flexibility of movement; muscles and tendons keep joints stable and move the bones. Locomotion requires energy. The energy is stored in the muscles (which contract and stretch to generate force) and in the elastic tendons as potential energy (stored energy), which is released as spring-like kinetic energy (the energy of motion) as the horse takes a step. Muscles and other body structures get the energy to do work both from food and from the oxygen that powers muscle cells. In the horse's limbs, the energy determines how well the horse moves, how much force it has available, how fast it can move, and how its different gaits function for optimal efficiency—using as little energy as possible for as long a time as possible.

In general, horses have four different gaits: the walk, trot, canter, and gallop. Scientists have studied each of these gaits and can explain the pattern of each and its usefulness to the horse. The walk is a four-beat gait in a predictable pattern of foot placement on the ground—left front foreleg, right hind leg, right foreleg, left hind leg. This is the horse's slowest, steadiest, most comfortable gait. It requires the least energy to maintain and keeps the energy cost of locomotion at a minimum. However, the faster a horse moves in a walking gait, the more energy it uses.

Gait, Energy, and Speed

When the walking gait becomes an inefficient use of energy, the horse begins to trot. In a trotting gait, the pattern of footfalls changes. A trot is a two-beat gait in which the horse springs from one diagonal to another. The first beat is the footfall of the right foreleg and the left hind leg. The second is the left foreleg and right hind leg. At one point in the pattern, all four of the horse's feet are off the ground; this is called suspension. The canter (faster than a trot) is a three-beat gait, with a kind of rocking motion. The horse's hooves may hit the ground in a pattern such as left hind leg, then right hind leg and left foreleg together, and then

The First Gait Analyst

In 1878 there was much disagreement over how horses moved during a race, because the gait patterns in racing horses could not be seen with the naked eye. Retired California governor Leland Stanford was a horse owner who believed that a running horse experienced a moment when all four feet were off the ground, and he wanted to prove it. At this point, cameras were primitive, and high-speed cameras were not even imagined, but Stanford persuaded the best photographer of the time, Eadweard Muybridge, to try to take photographs that would capture how horses run. At first, Muybridge thought the task impossible, but he finally figured out a way. He lined up twelve cameras that were aimed at a straight stretch of racing track, behind which a white backdrop was erected. Across the track, he strung twelve wires, each attached to a different camera. Muybridge filmed a trotter pulling a racing cart called a sulky. As the rapidly trotting horse tripped each wire, a camera shutter clicked, and Muybridge had twelve photos taken in half a second. For the first time ever, a photographer had clear, sharp images of the leg positions of a moving horse. Stanford was proved right in his theory, and the modern science of locomotion was born.

An Uncommon Farrier

Mike Stine is a farrier—a craftsman who cares for, trims, and shoes horses' hooves. He bought his first horse as a teenager in North Carolina and worked as a barn helper during high school to make money to care for the horse. He learned to ride and began to compete in Western events with his horse. As time passed, he became interested in horse-shoeing and took courses at a technical college to learn farrier skills. Stine became a professional farrier, and as he worked, he became more and more interested in horse locomotion and gait analysis. Today, Stine is a world-renowned expert on horse movement and biomechanics. He analyzes trotting and walking patterns and observes the back, shoulders, and joints, looking for unusual tensions or weaknesses. He uses his skills to correct movement problems, whether with the right kind of shoes or through an exercise program or by training the rider/owner to balance correctly. Stine says, "As a farrier, I strive to work with the entire horse to allow them to live a long comfortable life and reach their full potential in whatever activity we choose to participate."

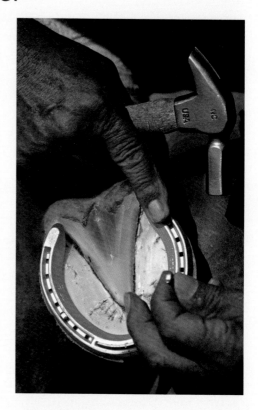

A farrier attaches a horseshoe to the hoof of a horse.

Quoted in Toni-Anne Collins. "Mike Stine the Journey-man Farrier." *The Cyberhorse Guide to Horse Health*, 2008. www.cyberhorse.net.au/cgi-bin/tve/displaynewsitem .pl?20080401mikestine.txt.

right foreleg. The fastest gait is the gallop. In this gait, the horse's two hind legs hit the ground almost together (with one just a split second behind the other) and the two fore-legs hit the ground together (with one slightly behind the other). Galloping horses also have a suspension time, or flight phase, in which all hooves are off the ground. A horse naturally uses these different gaits, depending on the speed at which it wants to move. Mathematics professor Ian Stewart says,

> So why do horses use different gaits at different speeds? It's a bit like the gears on a car. Patterns of movement that work fine at slow speeds become inefficient, or mechanically unworkable, at higher ones. To convince yourself of this, try walking faster and faster. At some point you will find that however hard you try, you don't speed up. But if you switch to a run, a different gait, going faster is suddenly easy. Experiments have revealed a close connection between a horse's gait, speed, and oxygen consumption. At low speeds, the walk uses [the] least oxygen. At higher speeds, the trot takes over. At higher speeds still, the gallop makes the best use of the available oxygen. However, the walk can be sustained for much longer than the trot, and the trot can be sustained for longer than the gallop—just as we can walk for longer periods than we can run.[14]

Each pattern of locomotion represents the optimal efficiency and energy conservation for the gait.

Some horses, particularly those used in the sport of harness racing, naturally have a fifth gait, called a pace. A pacer's gait is not diagonal, like the trot, but involves moving the front and back legs on each side together, right foreleg and hind leg and then left foreleg and hind leg. A pace is faster than a trot, and therefore, about 80 percent of horses involved in harness racing are pacers, while 20 percent are trotters. In harness racing, the horse must maintain a trot or pace throughout the race. If a horse breaks into a canter or a gallop in order to increase its speed, the horse is penalized or disqualified. Trotting and pacing are not the energy-efficient gaits for high speeds, so horses must be specifically trained not to break their gaits. In addition, most harness racing horses wear devices called hobbles, plastic loops or straps that connect the front and rear legs

TROT & GALLOP

A horse can breathe only in time with its stride, inhaling when its front hooves are reaching outward and exhaling only when all four legs come together.

BUILT FOR ENDURANCE

Certain physical characteristics make horse breeds such as Thoroughbreds and Arabians ideal for endurance events. Horses have large spleens that hold stores of oxygen-infused red blood cells. Red blood cells make up about 35 percent of the blood in humans during both rest and exercise, but in active horses the percentage can rise from 35 percent to 65 percent thanks to these stores. Racing breeds have higher proportions of slow-twitch muscle fibers, which convert the oxygen in these red blood cells to give the horse extra energy.

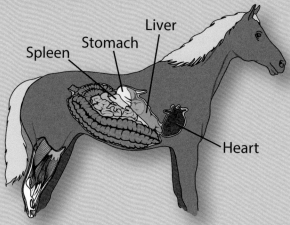

Liver

Stomach

Spleen

Heart

Muscle Types

Slow Twitch	Fast Twitch
Use oxygen for energy	Do not use oxygen for energy
Not ideal for fast movements	Best for rapid-fire movements
Do not tire easily	Tire quickly
Best for endurance sports	Best for short burst of activity

Oxygen-Rich Blood Cells

35% red blood cells

65% red blood cells

on the same side. The hobbles prevent the horse from switching its leg patterns to a more comfortable canter or gallop. Trotters do not wear hobbles, but they are much more likely to break stride when they try to move too fast. Both trotting and pacing are natural for horses, but maintaining the gaits at high speed is not, so harness races are much more difficult for horses than other kinds of racing.

The Biomechanical Competitive Edge

Not all horses are equal in their ability to use different gaits most efficiently, no matter the sport. In professional horse racing, obviously one Thoroughbred horse outraces all the others and wins. Gideon Ariel, a biomechanics expert, says, "For hundreds of years people have been asking 'what is it that makes one horse run faster than another.' This question is at the heart of biomechanics as applied to Thoroughbreds."[15] Ariel has studied the gaits of racehorses and determined several factors that identify the most efficient gallop. One important factor is the horse's stride length. Stride length is the distance of two placements (or pushes on the ground) of the same foot. Horses with greater stride lengths run the same distance faster than horses with shorter stride lengths. Another factor is called ground contact time. It is the amount of time that one hoof is in contact with the ground. Ariel explains, "The shorter the contact, the greater the magnitude of the force with which the horse pushes against the ground. For example, if a particular horse produces a contact time of 94 milliseconds, it is faster than one which has a 100 millisecond contact time."[16] The time that the horse remains airborne or suspended in the air with all four hooves off the ground affects speed, too. Since the horse cannot apply any force when in the air, a shorter airborne time means more time for hoof pushes on the ground and thus a faster horse.

THE HUGE FORCE OF GRAVITY

When an average-size horse lands after clearing a 2-foot (0.6m) jump, the force on its foot equals 3,156 pounds (1,431.5kg).

Some of the biomechanical systems of the horse that account for differences in galloping efficiency include the muscular strength in the horse's legs (especially its hind legs), the horse's size and length of its legs (for long strides), and the horse's conformation. Conformation refers to the balanced proportions of a horse's whole body. In a horse that is born balanced, for instance, the withers (the top of shoulder where the neck joins the body) are on the same level or slightly higher than the croup (the highest point from the rump to the top of the tail). In addition, since a horse uses its flexible back and neck muscles to change gaits or maintain gaits, the proportions of neck and back must be in balance, too. Veterinarian Christine Woodford explains, as an example, "If the neck is shorter than the horse's back, a horse tends to have decreased flexibility and a harder time balancing its motion. Longer-backed horses . . . have a harder time lifting, and rounding their backs, and moving their hindquarters underneath their center of gravity."[17] Balance and proportion are important because the horse's center of gravity affects its locomotion and biomechanical efficiency.

As seen in this photo of a jump, a horse's hind legs are nearly straight after the push to propel it off the ground.

Center of Gravity and Equestrian Success

The center of gravity is the point in the body around which the body's mass is evenly distributed. It is the point at which all the weight is concentrated, so that if supported there, a body remains in perfect balance. When an average horse is standing still, its center of gravity is at a point around its heart and deep in the center of its body. When a horse moves, however, its center of gravity shifts, and the horse must rebalance. A horse balances its body with its head and neck. If the horse does not rebalance effectively, its gait may be inefficient, and it may even injure itself and develop lameness as its stride length becomes uneven. In one study of racehorses, for example, Gideon Ariel discovered that some horses move their neck and back muscles too much vertically as they are galloping, while others keep the up and down movements of the back and neck to a minimum. Minimal vertical movements keep a horse's center of gravity more in balance and thus conserve energy. The horse that naturally is energy efficient is more likely to be a successful racehorse.

In jumping sports, however, it is not energy efficiency but rather vertical movement and the ability to rebalance the center of gravity that are essential for success. Just as a person throws his or her arms upward in order to raise the body's center of gravity to jump high, so does a horse reposition its body in order to jump. When a horse takes off over an obstacle, it shifts its center of gravity (and weight) backward by raising its head, shortening its neck, and lifting its shoulders. Shifting its weight backward enables the horse to lift its front legs off the ground and curl them in toward its body. Biomechanics expert Sheila Schils says, "This position makes the horse's body more streamlined so that less force is required to move the body over the fence."[18] With its weight shifted backward, the hind legs of the horse are compressed like a spring and this creates the energy with which the horse can propel itself up and forward over the fence. The back legs straighten out at the end of the push; it is a push with a force that is greater than the weight of

WORKING TOGETHER

During a jump, a rider crouches over the horse's body, as close to the horse's center of gravity as possible. This minimizes the work the horse must do to carry the rider, helping the horse successfully complete the jump.

A loose grip on the reins allows for head and neck movement.

The rider's center of gravity is positioned over the horse's.

Strong but relaxed muscles hold the rider in place.

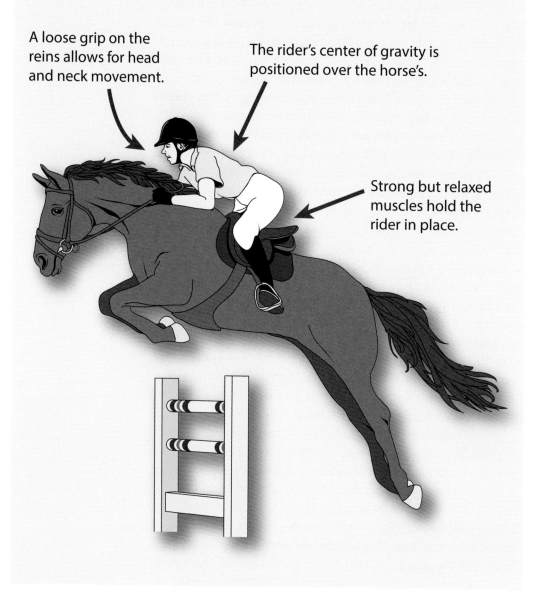

the horse's whole body. The horse's abdominal muscles and neck muscles help to pull its rear legs up and off the ground. In the beginning of the flight phase, the hind legs are straight backward, and the front legs are tightly curled. Then the horse begins to use its muscles to pull forward. It extends its neck and the whole front of its body and begins to bring its hind legs under its trunk.

At landing, the horse has to slow its momentum and reduce the force of impact with the ground. To begin slowing, the horse brings up its head and neck, again shifting its weight and center of gravity. The front legs hit the ground first, with one slightly ahead of the other. The front legs push against the ground, says Schils, "in an upward and backward direction."[19] Finally, the hind legs rotate completely underneath the horse's trunk and touch down just as the horse moves its front legs forward and out of the way. The whole sequence of body movement and muscular effort keeps the horse in balance, shifting its center of gravity throughout the jump and ensuring that the horse clears the obstacle.

Biomechanics and the Rider

A horse's rider must help the horse to maintain its balance by staying in balance with the horse's center of gravity. A human's center of gravity is located around the belly button, with his or her head being the heaviest body part. To stay in balance on a moving horse, the rider must resist the force of gravity and the horse's momentum by using his or her strong but relaxed muscles to resist the forces that pull the head forward or the body backward. The experienced rider balances his or her center of gravity over the horse's center of gravity, with the muscles relaxed so that the rider's body can move with the horse's movements. Then, since the horse shifts its center of gravity in order to jump, the rider's muscles must cooperate with the horse's muscular efforts. If he or she becomes out of balance, the horse's efforts are hindered. For example, as the horse takes off for the jump, moving its center of gravity forward, the rider has to shift position and move forward,

The jockey can improve the biomechanics of the horse during a race by crouching above the saddle. Jockey John Velazquez demonstrates this technique as he rides Animal Kingdom #16 to win the 2013 Kentucky Derby.

too, but not too far forward. A rider whose body leans too far forward ends up in front of the horse's center of gravity. Biomechanics professor Sian E.M. Lawson says, "This prevents the horse from raising its front end effectively (and puts him at risk of a fall)."[20] Another way that the rider may spoil the jump is to try to compensate for a loss of balance by lifting his or her hands and thus pulling on the reins. This action shortens the horse's neck and prevents the horse from stretching out to clear the obstacle and land safely. The result, says Lawson, can be that the horse, with its center of gravity shifted backward, cannot clear the obstacle with its hind end and hits the top of the fence with its back legs.

The strong, balanced rider makes a difference in horse racing, too. Until about 100 years ago, jockeys rode their Thoroughbreds sitting straight up in the saddle with their legs dangling straight down. Today, jockeys work harder during a race and use their muscles, and horses, in turn, run races some 5 to 7 percent faster than they did before. Incorporating principles of biomechanics, jockeys now stand in the stirrups, crouched low over their horse's center of gravity. The squatting position of the jockey saves energy for the horse by minimizing the work that its back muscles have to do. As it gallops, a horse's back muscles move up and down, or oscillate, to maintain its balance and its gait. With the jockey crouched above the saddle, the horse is spared the extra work of lifting him or her. Instead, the jockey's legs do the work. Physicist Andrew Spence explains, "Whether the jockey is sitting in the saddle or not, the horse still has to carry his weight. But by absorbing the jiggles of the horse, the jockey prevents the animal from having to make him go up and down with each stride. It's the difference between the horse carrying a moving rider or simply a quantity of lead that weighs the same."[21] As the work of the horse decreases, the work of the rider increases, but the trade-off means optimal performance for the team. The perfectly balanced horse-and-rider system means the best chance for success in every equestrian sport.

CHAPTER 4

The Environmental Factors of Equestrian Sports

E ven a perfectly balanced horse-and-rider team is not guaranteed success in equestrian sports. That is because no horse and rider compete under ideal or perfectly identical conditions, even in the same event. Varying environmental factors, such as weather conditions, performance surfaces, and riding tack (saddles, bridles, bits, and other equipment), can affect the biomechanics and physics that determine how well the team performs. In some equestrian sports, the variable environmental factors are under human control, but sometimes both horse and rider must simply deal with differing conditions that occur naturally on the day of the sporting event.

The Saddle

One of the most important ways that a rider can work with the horse and help it perform its best is the choice of tack. Different saddles, for example, are used in different sports, but each must fit the horse well. Saddle maker and fitter Danny Kroetch says that there are nineteen points at which a saddle can cause pressure on the horse's back. He says that since horses are individuals, the saddle has to be custom-fit to a particular horse at all these points in order for the horse to be balanced and comfortable when it is perform-

ing. Chrisann Ware, a saddle fitter and equine therapist, explains, "There is a vast range of difference in the shape of horses' backs even between horses of the same breeds. You must treat each horse individually. It doesn't matter which style of saddle you choose, what does matter is that the tree [base of the saddle] and underside of the saddle is a mirror image of your horse's back and that the saddle is soft enough to bend and flex slightly with the horse's movements."[22] Otherwise, where the saddle fits poorly, it creates pressure at one or more points on the horse's back, and this pressure leads to soreness.

Colorful saddles are on display at a horse show in the French Pyrenees. Riders should choose a saddle that is proper to the sport or activity and that is the right fit for the individual horse.

A sore horse tries to protect its back muscles by relaxing its stomach muscles to force its back downward. Horse experts call this hollowing the back. The result can be a loss of range of motion, pressure of muscles on the nerves that causes more pain, back muscle weakness, and an asymmetry of the back instead of balance. An ill-fitting saddle and a hollow back affect the biomechanics of the horse no matter what its sport. Ware says, "Whether horses are dancing lightly in the dressage arena or powering across the cross country course the biomechanics of good movement are all the same."[23] Protecting the muscles from pain helps to ensure good movement in the horse.

The Rider and the Right Saddle

As both a doctor and an expert dressage competitor, Max Gahwyler says that a well-fitting saddle is as important for the rider as it is for the horse. Gahwyler's saddles are custom-made for him. Each saddle fits the horse's back comfortably and keeps Gahwyler in perfect balance, too. Gahwyler's dressage saddle suits the length of his thighs and legs so that he can bend his legs. He says that riders who stretch their legs downward are forced to sit on their crotches, and this means that they cannot use their bodies to communicate with their horses and are off-balance. Gahwyler says every saddle should be built to suit the individual rider's hips, pelvis, and legs. He explains, "Whenever a saddle fails to conform to the rider's body shape, there will be problems that are then blamed on the horse."

Quoted in Heather Smith Thomas. "Dressage Saddle Fit Importance." Equisearch.com (From *Dressage Today* magazine). www.equisearch.com/horses_riding_training /english/dressage/saddlefit_081904.

Saddle Choices for Different Sports

The weight of the saddle affects a horse's performance in many sports, too, since added weight inevitably slows down the horse. The heaviest saddles are Western saddles, which are designed to be comfortable for the rider when he or she is riding for many hours at a time. The Western saddle evenly distributes the weight of the rider and saddle on the horse's back, and this helps both horse and rider to maintain a center of gravity. In barrel racing, however, the weight can be a hindrance, so special barrel racing Western saddles have been developed. The seat is deep, to help the rider stay seated and in balance with the horse's center of gravity during sharp turns at high speeds, but these saddles are generally made to weigh no more than about 30 pounds (13.6kg). The Western saddle used in roping events, however, may weigh as much as 50 pounds (22.7kg) because the stability of saddle, horse, and rider is most important in these sports.

English saddles, used in sports such as dressage, show jumping, and polo, are smaller and lighter than Western saddles. English saddles weigh about 15 to 20 pounds (6.8 to 9kg). They are designed to allow the horse the greatest freedom of movement and to keep the horse comfortable. The seat of the saddle is shallow to allow the rider flexibility of movement and close body contact with the horse. With

A light English saddle, such as the one in this photo, is used in sports including dressage, show jumping, and polo.

an English saddle, both horse and rider can communicate through their muscles and be aware of each other's movements. The lightest of all saddles is the jockey's saddle in Thoroughbred racing, because the less weight a horse carries, the faster it can run. The jockey's saddle is just a small patch on the horse's back. It has no seat, because the jockey does not sit at all during the race, and it weighs between 12 ounces and 6 pounds (0.3 to 2.7kg).

No matter what the saddle, its placement on the horse's back affects the sport. Ideally, explains Chrisann Ware, the saddle would be placed so that the rider sits exactly over the horse's center of gravity, but this is not possible. That positioning would require placing the weight of the rider and saddle very far forward and on the horse's relatively thin shoulder muscles. The horse would be bruised and injured by the pressure, and the rider would be unbalanced and at risk of a fall. Ware says about saddle placement, "We must compromise between what is best for weight carrying and what is anatomically possible without causing damage."[24]

In the sport of dressage the rider uses the bit and bridle to imperceptibly direct the horse's actions.

Saddles are generally placed on the back over the horse's shelf of ribs—as close as possible to the horse's center of gravity but right behind the shoulder. In this position, the rider is most balanced and comfortable, too. He or she sits easily in the deepest part of the saddle with legs spread on each side of the horse in a relaxed posture, moving in time with the horse's movements. Still, no saddle position is perfect and no saddle fits absolutely perfectly. Saddles are artificial objects and they never help the horse to perform. They are there to benefit the rider, and the horse that copes best with the effect of the saddle on its natural biomechanics is the horse that performs best in its sport.

TROT & GALLOP

Many riders use safety saddle stirrups that are designed to prevent their feet from being caught in the stirrup in a fall. The stirrups break away or open up so the rider falls free and will not be dragged with one foot pinned in the stirrup if the horse keeps moving.

The Effect of Bits and Bridles

Bits and bridles are also artificial aids, including reins and mouthpieces, which are used by riders to control and direct their mounts, whether to steer them to the next jump or guide them through a group of racing horses. While such equipment can hinder a horse's natural movements, it can aid in the horse's responsiveness to the rider's wishes. Some uses of bridles and bits, however, are not without controversy, especially in the sport of dressage. At the level of Olympic competition, horses are required to wear a double bridle with two bits for the horse's mouth. The double bridle gives the rider more control over the horse's movements than standard bridles. In dressage, judges award points for the elegance of the movements and positions of the horse, while the rider appears to sit unmoving and signals the horse with the slightest of movements. With a double bridle, the rider, with almost imperceptible pulling on the reins, can direct the horse into trained postures, such as a trot with exaggerated leg lifts or an elegantly posed head. While the movement of the reins is slight, however, the pressure of the bits in the horse's mouth is exaggerated. This pressure, some critics say, is a form of abuse that causes unnecessary pain for the horse. With the pressure, which the horse attempts to avoid by pulling in its neck and head, a beautiful posture is achieved. The practice is called *rollkur*, a German word that means "flexion [bending] of the horse's neck achieved through aggressive force."[25]

In 2010, the Fédération Equestre Internationale (FEI) banned the use of *rollkur* in Olympic events after public outrage over an apparent abuse of a dressage horse in 2009. The horse's rider, Patrik Kittel, was videotaped using *rollkur* while warming up his horse for an event. The horse's tongue had turned blue and was hanging out of his mouth. The FEI prohibits prolonged or excessive flexing of a horse's neck during its events, but critics argue that the practice of *rollkur* is still common, either during an event or during the warm-up before an event in order to threaten the horse and make it flex its neck in expectation of the pressure and

Riders compete in the 2013 Preakness Stakes. Horses riding closely behind others encounter less wind resistance.

LOSING FRICTION AND RISKING INJURY

A combination of forces interacts to make a horse's movement around a racetrack possible. When a hoof pushes down and back on the ground a reaction force pushes back, and the friction created by the rough ground surface moving past the hoof's surface keeps the hoof from slipping, and allows the horse to push against the ground and move forward. If a horse runs across an icy patch, however, there is little or no friction to stop the hoof's backward movement and the horse may slip and fall, risking serious injury.

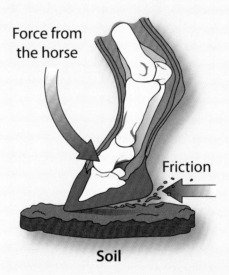

Force from the horse

Friction

Soil

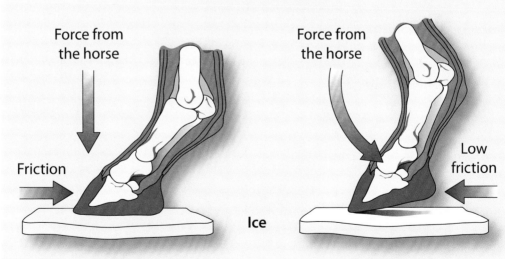

Force from the horse

Friction

Ice

Force from the horse

Low friction

pain during the event itself. German veterinarian Gerd Heuschmann says that *rollkur* interferes with a horse's correct biomechanics and restricts its airway, and he and many other dressage participants and horse experts reject the practice. Some people involved in the sport, like sisters and dressage trainers Camille and Gabrielle Dareau, even argue that double bridles should not be allowed at all in dressage competitions. Nevertheless, the use of double bridles and the opportunity they allow for abuse are today a common part of the sport of dressage. It is one instance of a sport in which the rider may win by using an artificial item that works to the horse's detriment.

The Larger Environment: Air Resistance

Usually, environmental factors that work to the horse's detriment are undesirable in equestrian events, but are out of the rider's control. Wind and air resistance, for example, can have a large effect on horse races. Air resistance is also called drag. It is the force that pushes back on a moving object and acts in opposition to the motion of any solid object

A horse gets a bath after a workout to help it cool down.

as it moves through the air. Air resistance increases as velocity increases, and the drag requires energy to overcome. Because of air resistance and drag, a galloping racehorse is slowed down and therefore needs more energy to run the same distance than if there was no air to fight against. According to science writer Achim Eberhart, in a typical race approximately 17 percent of a horse's energy is used up fighting drag.

Jockeys know that air resistance is a factor in winning races, and so they practice drafting, or "covering up," to increase their chances of winning. The horse that leads the pack throughout most of the race, especially during the final leg, often turns out not to be the winner, because it gets tired and slows down. A horse running with the pack, however, can run in the slipstream of any horse it is closely following. The slipstream is the area of reduced pressure and drag directly behind a moving object. This is why NASCAR drivers like to race directly behind another car or why migrating geese fly in a vee formation behind one another—the air resistance is less for those in the rear than for those in front. Similarly, a jockey who keeps his horse slipstreaming is saving the horse's energy for a final spurt of speed in the last leg of the race. British scientist Andrew Spence conducted a study of more than forty-five hundred races over a two-year period and discovered that covering up made a big difference in racing outcomes. He says, "When measured over the entire race, the average speed of a horse goes up the more time it spends tucked in behind other horses. If you convert that difference in speed into how the horse finishes, it can amount to a gain of three to four places."[26]

Air resistance increases when wind pressure increases, so the stronger the wind is blowing, the more effect it has on the outcome of a race. Handicappers (people who predict the outcomes of races) look at weather reports as one determination of race winners and racing speeds. Horse races are run on oval tracks, so a race may begin with the horses galloping into the wind but end with the horses galloping with the wind behind them. This situation may lead to a slow start but a fast finish. Since the blowing wind at the

Extreme Horse Racing

Every winter, on the ice of the frozen lake of St. Moritz, Switzerland, Thoroughbreds and jockeys engage in the White Turf horse races. The horses wear special horseshoes studded with spikes. Jockeys wear ski goggles and face masks. Different races are held over three consecutive weeks. Jockeys ride their horses in flat races, compete in trotting races, and—most unusual of all—race in the skijoring. Skijoring is a race in which skiers are dragged behind barebacked, riderless horses. Some people worry that the races are cruel to the horses, but others insist that the horses have so much fun that they are hard to stop when the race is over.

One trainer, Christian von der Recke, says that the only problem is the cold. He says, "Some horses don't like it that cold. And obviously there are problems breathing up here [in the high mountains]. You can never tell beforehand which horse likes it up here and which doesn't. You can only bring them here." No one can predict which horses will be willing to race or which horses will win because the conditions are so extreme, and it is the only race like it in the world.

Quoted in Simon Bradley. "Galloping in a Winter Wonderland." SwissInfo.ch, February 19, 2010. www .swissinfo.ch/eng/sport/Galloping_in_a_winter_won derland.html?cid=8332660

Skiers participate in the skijoring at the 2007 White Turf race on Lake St. Moritz, Switzerland.

finish helps the lead horse run faster, the handicapper may predict that the leading horse will win. If the wind directions are reversed, however, and the horses are running into the wind at the end of the race, a horse that has drafted with the pack is more likely to have the energy to fight the wind and win the race.

Weather and Heat

Air temperature, especially heat, is another environmental factor that affects equestrian sports. Like people, horses sweat through their skin to cool off, but they do not cool off as easily as people do. Michael Lindinger, a Canadian scientist, explains that hot weather can raise an exercising horse's body temperature up to ten times faster than a person's, leading to heat stress, dehydration, and serious injury to its internal organs. For a horse, sweating is not efficient enough in hot weather to cool down its body temperature when it is participating in an active sport. Lindinger explains that only about 30 percent of the horse's sweat evaporates and cools the horse. He says, "Because so much more sweat is produced than can be evaporated, the rest just drips off the horse's body. By comparison, up to 50 percent of the sweat people produce is evaporated from our bodies during exercise and helps to cool us."[27] Horses also lose salts when they sweat, and Lindinger says that a horse's sweat is four times saltier than human sweat. This means that the horse is at great risk for illness or even death in a short amount of time unless the salts are replaced.

Because horses have a difficult time regulating body temperature and salts when they exercise heavily on hot days, sport horses may have to be protected from undue exertion. Heat is most likely to endanger horses in high-speed races or in long-distance races. In both cases, the horses expend a great deal of energy, generate body heat, and must be able to cool down their bodies. Because of this, Thoroughbred races are occasionally canceled to protect the horses' health. In Toronto, Canada, in 2011, for example, races were canceled when temperatures of 100°F (37.8°C) and high humidity were predicted.

TROT & GALLOP

On muddy tracks, jockeys wear many layers of clear film on their visors. As the mud is splattered on their faces, the jockeys just peel off a layer at a time so that they can see what they are doing without having to wipe off the visors.

Even under normal warm weather temperatures, horses racing over long distances can suffer heat stress. Endurance racing, for instance, is a demanding, long-distance sport in which horses can be dangerously stressed by air temperature during the event. Endurance horses race over a trail of 50 to 100 miles (80.5 to 161km) in a single day. The natural result of this heavy exercise is increased sweating and salt loss. Lindinger tells a story of a cross-country endurance competition that took place one hot day. At a required veterinary inspection stop along the way, the horses were all scraped of sweat and cooled with water. After all the horses had continued the race and the water left on the ground had evaporated, someone took a photograph of the area. The ground was completely white from the salt of the horses' sweat. Because of the excessive demands on a horse's body during endurance races, the sport's regulations require that all horses be checked by a veterinarian at the beginning of the event, at a series of "holds" or inspection stops along the way, and at the end of the race. To protect the horse's health and safety, the veterinarian pulls from the competition any horse so stressed that it cannot pass the check. Only about 40 percent of horses are able to finish any particular endurance event.

Mud and the Racetrack

Another weather factor that may affect a horse's performance is the condition of the racing surface. Track condition is particularly important in Thoroughbred racing events, and while the track may be affected by past weather—fair, clear days or rain prior to the race, for example—conditions caused by this kind of weather do not stop racing events. Racing tracks are usually grass or dirt, but sometimes these tracks are dry and sometimes they are wet and sloppy. Each condition can affect a horse's performance. Dry tracks usually yield the fastest race finishes. Wet, muddy tracks mean slower races. Each hoof push of the horse sinks into the soft ground, and the horse may slip and slide, unable to gain traction in the mud.

Under muddy conditions, the horse that takes the lead early often wins—no horse ahead of it is kicking mud in its face, and it is difficult for horses in the back of the pack to put on a burst of speed at the end of the race. Some horses, called mudders, may also just cope better with sloppy conditions. Some horse experts believe that horses with large feet do better in mud; others believe that horses that naturally take high strides do best, even when they have small feet; some say that the actual weight of the mud thrown on a horse and jockey can slow them down enough to lose the race. Many admit that they do not know all the factors that may influence a horse's ability or willingness to cope with different environments.

Environmental factors in equestrian sports can test the skill of the horse-and-rider team, but they are also tests of each horse's build, conformation, and personality. For the equestrian, this means trying to choose the horse that is best for each individual sport.

CHAPTER 5

The Right Horse for the Sport

lmost since the first horses were domesticated, humans have tried to improve upon nature and breed the perfect horse for human needs. For hundreds of years, long before they understood the genetics involved, people bred horses for different tasks. The result is that today there are more than three hundred distinct breeds around the world. Modern breeders continue the tradition of trying to develop the perfect horse for each sport and often use the science of genetics to understand why some horses outperform others and to improve on individual horse lines within breeds.

Selective Breeding

A breed is a group of horses with common origins and with characteristics not found in other groups that are reliably passed on to the offspring. No one knows when the first horse breeds were developed, but many theorize that the Arabian is among the oldest breeds in the world. Originating with the bedouin people of the Arabian Peninsula, the breed is known for its cooperative, affectionate nature toward humans; intelligence; eagerness to please; and high spirits. Physically, it is recognized by its long, arched neck and a hip and leg conformation suited for agility and rac-

ing. Arabians are one of the top ten most popular horse breeds and are the most common horses used in endurance sports.

Like other kinds of horses, Arabians were developed through a process called selective breeding. Selective breeding is the artificial selection (by humans) of the animals that are allowed to reproduce. Over time and generations of horses, for example, a naturally cooperative nature became a trait of Arabian horses because only cooperative horses were allowed to mate and bear foals. Since wild-acting, unresponsive horses were never bred, that trait died out in the breed. Selective breeding, in many different parts of the world, eventually led to major changes in the types of horses that humans domesticated. Different breeds were also bred to each other in order to produce new breeds. This was the process by which Thoroughbreds came to be. They are a product of a cross between three Arabian stallions and a larger number of English mares that were bred together, with the offspring then bred together for generations, during the seventeenth and eighteenth centuries in England.

An Arabian horse owned by a Saudi prince performs at a 2012 horse show in Sharjah, United Arab Emirates. The Arabian breed is one of the oldest and has helped shape almost all modern riding breeds.

Breed "Blood" Groups

Modern horse breeds are generally categorized into three groups: hot bloods, cold bloods, and warm bloods. "Blood" refers not to blood temperature, since all horses have the same body temperature, but to the temperament of the horse breed and the kinds of jobs to which they are suited. Hot-blooded horses are athletic, agile, and spirited. They may be affectionate and cooperative with people, but they can be fiery in temperament and sensitive to environmental stimuli. Their bodies are built for speed and endurance, but they are relatively lightweight, with delicate, slender legs and lean, streamlined bodies. Thoroughbreds and Arabians are hot-blooded horses and are the breeds most often chosen for racing.

Cold-blooded horses are the heavier breeds with calm, stable natures and physical strength and stamina. They have strong legs and heavy bodies. Traditionally, the cold-blooded breeds are used for work such as hauling timber, pulling heavy wagons, or plowing fields. Breeds in this category include Clydesdales, Percherons, Belgians, Shires, and Welsh ponies. Their size can range from quite small to giant, reaching 6 feet (1.8m) in height. Most cold bloods are not suitable for sports, except perhaps in hauling or pulling competitions.

Warm-blooded horses are a mixture of cold bloods and hot bloods and have traits from both groups. They are not as high-strung and fast as hot bloods, nor as heavy and slow as cold bloods, but they have the intelligence, energy, strength, and agility to perform in many situations. Examples of warm bloods include quarter horses, Lipizzaners, American Standardbreds, Missouri Fox Trotters, Appaloosas, Hanoverians, and Hackneys. Warm-blooded horses are often the choice for such equestrian sports as dressage, Western events, endurance events, and show jumping.

Many good riding horses are mixed breed, but in equestrian sports it is important to choose the horse best suited

TROT & GALLOP

A pony is a breed of horse that measures less than 14.2 hands high. (One hand is equal to 4 inches or 10.16 centimeters.)

Clydesdales are categorized as cold blooded horses. The breed was developed in the nineteenth century for pulling heavy loads.

to the sport. Breeds determine traits and characteristics, such as trainability or physical skills or conformation. That is why most horse breeders use careful selective breeding to keep the breed pure and to try to ensure the most perfect breed example in any offspring. Horses are individuals, and not every characteristic can be selectively bred into the next generations, but inheritance and genetics play a critical role in determining how well a breed of horse or a specific individual performs in any given sport. Many traits and characteristics are determined by the genes.

Which Breed?

Although many breeds of horses are adaptable for different sports, competitive riders try to choose the best horse for the sport. Thoroughbreds are best suited to professional racing, but they also compete in dressage, show jumping, and eventing. The American quarter horse is ridden in Western events, such as sprint racing, rodeos, barrel racing, and roping competitions. Arabians are good at endurance events, as are Missouri Fox Trotters; and Standardbreds are often one of the breeds preferred for harness racing. In dressage, some of the breeds chosen at the Olympic level of competition include the Andalusian, the Danish Warmblood, and the Hanoverian. The best show jumpers include many breeds also good for dressage, as well as the Appaloosa, Belgian and Dutch Warmbloods, Holsteiner, and Westphalian. The popularity of different breeds for different sports can change, too. For example, although it is not an actual breed, the Argentine polo pony—a cross between the Thoroughbred and the criollo (a breed of Argentina)—is fast becoming the preferred horse for competitive polo.

How Horse Genetics Works

In the nucleus of almost every cell in the bodies of all living organisms are spiraled coils of deoxyribonucleic acid (DNA). DNA carries the genetic instructions—the blueprint for the cell's functioning—that controls how the cell and ultimately the body are structured and operate. In horses, the DNA is arranged into thirty-two pairs of chromosomes, and each chromosome is made up of thousands of genes. Genes are specific sequences of DNA or units of heredity. Most genes are the same for all horses; they are what make horses into horses, humans into humans, and mice into mice. Some genetic instructions, however, are unique to each individual and to each breed of horse. These instructions are inherited by the horse from its parents—

GENETIC RECOMBINATION AND CHROMOSOMAL CROSSOVER

Genetic recombination in the form of chromosomal crossover occurs when an individual's reproductive cells (eggs or sperm) are being created. During this process, unpaired strands of maternal and paternal DNA (known as chromosomes) replicate and then exchange some of their genetic material. These altered chromosomes are then passed on to the individual's offspring. Genetic recombination ensures genetic variety in a species and can lead to the development of unique traits and characteristics.

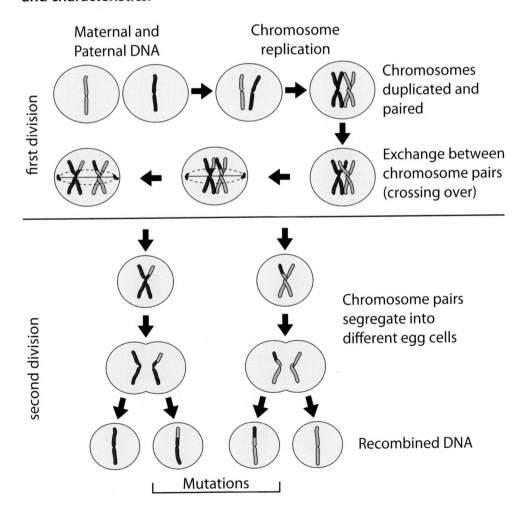

half from the egg of the mother and half from the sperm of the father. The egg and sperm cells have only half the chromosomes of other cells in the body. They are formed when a parent cell in the mother or father's body splits into two identical cells. During the process of division (a special kind of cell division called meiosis, in which the nucleus duplicates itself and divides), each newly-duplicated chromosome is lined up beside its double. Sections of the duplicate chromosomes then intertwine and exchange DNA with each other. This biologic process, called recombination, ensures that the genetic information in each fertilized egg will be unique, and this is why every individual horse is different from every other. The fertilized egg from which the horse developed combines all thirty-two chromosome pairs and grows by cell division, or mitosis, until it becomes a fetus and then a newborn foal. The baby has inherited genetic information from both parents but is never identical to either parent.

Within its chromosomes, the foal carries the pairs of genes (one from each parent) that often determine traits. Each half of the pair is an alternate form of the gene, called an allele, which can be slightly different in coding but influences the same traits or characteristics. Different alleles can have varying degrees of penetrance, meaning whether the trait carried by the gene is manifested by the individual. In the simplest form of inheritance, alleles can be dominant or recessive. An example of simple dominant/recessive inheritance is a rare genetic disease in Arabian horses called severe combined immunodeficiency disease (SCID). Foals born with this disease have no immune system to protect them from catching diseases, and they die from infections within the first three months of life.

According to the Horse Genome Project—a group of scientists working to map the genome (DNA sequence) of the domestic horse—about 8 percent of Arabians have one allele for this disease. The gene pair of these animals includes one normal allele and one SCID allele. However, the horses are healthy because the normal allele is dominant. An article from the Horse Genome Project explains, "SCID is caused by a recessive gene. This means that affected foals inherit a copy of the gene from both parents. Horses with one copy of the gene are unaffected and [are] called carriers."[28] Both parents must be a carrier of the disease for a foal to have SCID, and whether a foal inherits both SCID alleles is dependent on chance. Half of the time, the foal will inherit one normal and one SCID allele and become a carrier; 25 percent of the time it inherits two dominant normal copies; and 25 percent of the time it will inherit both recessive SCID alleles and will be born with the disease. In 1997, the recessive gene that causes SCID was identified, and a DNA blood test was developed so that horses can now be tested to see if they are carriers. Arabian breeders are

On the Genetic Trail

Veterinarian Stephanie Valberg is a member of the Horse Genome Project and director of the Equine Center at the University of Minnesota. A career as a genetic researcher has allowed her to pursue her life-long interests in scientific research and horses. Valberg has developed blood tests for identifying some genetic diseases and has identified the genetic mutations that cause other diseases. In one disease in quarter horses, called GBED, an inherited genetic mutation prevents the horse's muscle cells from converting glucose to glycogen and thus the animal has no fuel for energy or for body organ functioning. The disease is always fatal early in life. With DNA testing, Valberg found the mutated recessive gene in quarter horse foals that causes GBED. She then used her detective skills to trace the ancestry of animals with GBED and discovered that all the animals were related through one stallion named King, born in 1932.

An increase in inherited diseases is one problem with mating animals in a small, breed-specific pool of individuals (hundreds or thousands). It means that over time, related animals that carry recessive genes end up being bred together and pass dangerous alleles to their offspring.

attempting to improve the health of the horse breed with this genetic tool.

Genes and Selective Breeding

Most traits are not inherited as simply as SCID. Many traits are determined by multiple genes. In addition, the DNA coding of the genes can change when the chromosomes are dividing to copy themselves or when the genes are being shuffled around during recombination. When a gene's coding is altered, scientists call this a mutation. Every organism has errors in its DNA coding, and usually the mistakes are of no consequence. Sometimes, however, the mistakes cause diseases, and other times they are desirable.

Mutations and allele variations help explain how new breeds are developed. The scientists of the Horse Genome Project believe that coat color, for instance, was probably the first use of genetics by people when they domesticated horses. The scientists say about color:

A technician at an equine reproduction center in Argentina processes the semen from a stud horse for breeding.

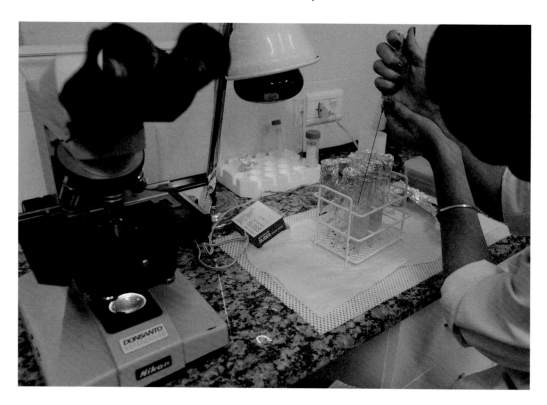

We are just now identifying the genes responsible for the different color patterns. There is one gene that determines whether a horse produces black pigment or only red pigment in its hairs. Another gene determines whether that black will occur throughout the body or be restricted to the mane, tail and legs. There are several genes that dilute the red or black coat pigments to create palomino, buckskin, silver and other colors. There are several genes that produce white hairs in distinctive patterns that we call overo, tobiano, sabino or white. Several genes interact to produce the various white hair patterns we call appaloosa. A gene called grey will cause all colored hairs to turn white as the horse ages.[29]

Variations and mutations explain the diverse colors in different horse breeds and are maintained by breeders who mate together only the horses within the breed that have the correct color. Lipizzaner horses, for example, which were bred for dressage, are pure white because the original breeders selectively bred for that color. In other breeds, colors may vary because color is not an important consideration for the breed. Thoroughbreds, for instance, come in many solid colors, but the traits that matter to breeders are conformation and temperament. Humans practice selective breeding for these traits in an effort to breed for performance, just as historically, people bred for color. The breed is kept pure by breeders who keep careful records of each animal's parentage and ancestry, which can be traced back to other horses of the same breed.

But Which Horse Inherited the Winning Genes?

Even in purebred animals, however, scientists cannot identify as yet the specific genes that determine the most desirable traits of sport horses. Thoroughbreds have a predictable general conformation and temperament, but the degree to which any individual Thoroughbred excels in these areas is unpredictable. The individual's conformation determines its shape, proportions, movements, and physical performance, but what determines the best conformation is complex. Breeders cannot create the perfect foal, even by mating two parents with excellent conformation. Geneticist Glynis Giddings explains, "In reality horse conformation is the combination of many traits (characters), each influenced by different genes and also affected by the environment, especially during development."[30] Horses are born true to their breed, exhibiting the characteristics specific to that breed, but there is so much individual variability in horses within breeds that no one can determine which Thoroughbred will be a winning racehorse.

Determining which horse has the genes to become a winner became more plausible, however, in 2010, when Irish scientist Emmeline Hill and her research team identified a gene in Thoroughbreds that has been named the speed gene. This gene codes for the size of muscle cells. Variations in this gene seem to determine whether a horse is most suited for short-distance sprints, medium-distance races, or long-distance events. Hill calls the allele for sprinting the C allele, and the allele for long-distance running the T allele. Horses tested by Hill that inherited two C alleles (one from each parent) turned out to be the best sprinters. Horses with two T alleles were the best long-distance racers. Horses with one C allele and one T allele did best with middle-distance racing. Using a DNA test developed by Hill and her colleagues, breeders are now able to test both male and female parents and foals for which variants they carry. This means that breeders will know the kind of racing to which a foal is suited or how to selectively breed parents in order to get a foal that is best suited to a desired kind of racing.

The speed gene is the first gene ever identified that is at least partly responsible for an athletic trait in Thoroughbreds. The discovery of such genes could forever change the practice of selective breeding. Hill says of her discovery,

TROT & GALLOP

A purebred horse is one that has two parents of the same breed. A cross is a horse with two parents of known but different breeds. A grade is a horse of unknown parentage.

Breeding techniques for Thoroughbred horses have remained relatively unchanged for centuries. Breeders currently rely on combining successful bloodlines together, hoping that the resulting foal will contain that winning combination of genes. Until now, whether those winning genes have or have not been inherited could only be surmised by observing the racing and breeding success of a horse over an extended period of years after its birth.[31]

Now, Hill believes, breeding decisions can be based on science, and in the future, as more gene variants are discovered, selective breeding will be based on the genetic profiles of the parents.

This kind of genetic knowledge could someday clearly

Teri Lear, an equine geneticist, grooms Desert Heir in 2007. They both participate in the Horse Genome Project, an international effort to define the DNA sequence of the domestic horse.

identify potential equestrian winners. Like Hill and her colleagues, geneticist Steven Tammariello has also developed a test for three different genes that may affect a Thoroughbred's racing ability. One of the genes helps code for energy production, which affects a horse's stamina. The other two code for functioning of the muscles. These two genes code for a phenomenon called muscle twitch. Muscle twitch that is slow helps a horse have power, while fast muscle twitching is related to speed. Tammariello has tested for variants of muscle twitch genes in several different breeds of horses. He reports, "We found a gene variant that is in high frequency in draft horses that was also found in slow Thoroughbreds. Many of our clients have brood mares and they want to know whether they carry the variant for slower muscle twitch. Slower twitch is useful for muscular power, but not for speed. We can test a group of Thoroughbreds and predict which ones have the worst chance to make it to the track."[32]

Genetic profiling, Tammariello says, will never produce the perfect horse, because genetic tests alone cannot identify perfect horse genes or change the genes with which a horse is born. He explains that there is no way to produce "superhorses," but says there may be a way to avoid breeding for genetic flaws. He adds, "We wanted to improve the chance of horses running well. . . . If you have a good idea of what you will get, you may forgo breeding horses that have a high probability of producing foals that may fail as racehorses."[33] Tammariello also says that he could research and discover the gene variants that make the best jumpers or the best polo ponies, and he believes that such knowledge would improve the breeding methods, health, and soundness for all sport horses.

Beyond the Genes

Genes, however, are only one part of what makes a successful sport horse. How a horse is treated, how it is trained, and what kind of experiences it has had throughout its life all play a role in the making of an individual. Intangible qualities such as talent, the will to win, or eagerness to please are just not predictable, even when genetics and environment are considered together. Sports writer Ben Baugh sums up this view of the most successful horses when he says, "There is no yardstick, barometer, gauge, level measurement or tape measure when it comes to determining the size of an athlete's heart."[34]

CHAPTER 6

Training, Conditioning, and Nutrition

No matter how well it may be bred or how optimal its genetic heritage, a horse cannot become a successful athlete without training and good physical care. In equestrian sports, the rider requires conditioning and training, too. Both members of the athletic partnership need optimal physical health and fitness if the team is to succeed.

The First Lessons

The training of a horse really begins with its mother from the moment of the foal's birth. With both sound and touch, the mother shapes the foal's behavior as it imprints on the mare and learns to trust and follow her lead. Imprinting is the psychological process by which a newborn animal, during the early, critical period of its life, forms an attachment to its mother and begins to pattern its behavior after hers. Foals imprint on or bond with their mothers, and many horse breeders and trainers say that this bonding can occur between human and foal, too. These experts practice a method called imprint training, believing that a foal can imprint on its mother and a human at the same time.

Imprint training, according to its developer, veterinarian Robert M. Miller, is the way to ensure that a foal's personality is permanently shaped within hours of its birth so that

it grows up to be a well-mannered, responsive, and easily handled horse. The method is detailed and complex, but, in general, it requires that the breeder hold the foal as soon as it is born and rub it all over, first with a towel and then with the hands, while the foal is gently but firmly restrained. The process teaches the foal to submit to human leadership since it is held and rubbed until it completely relaxes and accepts human handling and dominance. At the same time, the foal is imprinting on the human, becoming dependent on the human imprinter, and bonding with him or her. Veterinarian Robert N. Oglesby explains, "Following this procedure the foal is compliant, accepting of human companionship, and easily led and trained. Dr. Miller says this imprinting is permanent and results in an unafraid but respectful foal."[35]

Not all horse breeders and trainers accept imprint training. Some believe that it is more natural to leave the mother and foal alone for a few days so as not to interfere with the bond between the two. Others wait until the foal is being

A Thoroughbred breeder trains a five-day-old foal alongside its mother with a halter and bridle and lead rope.

Being a Horse Trainer

In the Thoroughbred horse racing world, top horse trainers are admired and respected, but it takes many years of experience and much knowledge of horses to be successful. Horse trainers are responsible for the feeding and training of all the horses in the stable. They develop exercise schedules for the horses and schedule races that suit the individual horse's ability level. Trainers hire the jockeys and manage the grooms, farriers, and barn workers. Trainers watch for any physical problems in the horses and consult with veterinarians and nutrition specialists whenever necessary. In addition, they are experts in horse conformation and heritage and accompany owners to horse sales to provide advice about which horses to buy. As a rule, trainers start at the bottom and work their way up, learning as they go. Famous trainer Nick Zito, for example, began his career when he was a teen as a hot walker—walking horses after exercise or races to cool them down. He moved up to being an assistant groomer and then was an assistant trainer for four years before he became a trainer on his own. After years of work and dedication, Zito became a top trainer of Kentucky Derby winners.

weaned from the mother, thinking that the foal at that time will welcome a human companion and become attached to the human because it has lost the bond with its mother. Whenever the human breeder begins interacting with the foal, however, the goals are approximately the same: The horse must be safe for people to handle, responsive to human guidance, and able to perform usefully. Practically, this means teaching the foal to trust and not fear humans; to submit to the human as it would to its mother and later to the herd leader; to accept human touch and learn to be guided by touch; and to calmly accept normal sounds, sights, and other stimulation that occur in the human environment.

During its first year of life, a foal is also taught to accept and wear a halter and a bridle, to follow a lead rope, to submit to grooming procedures, and to begin to work at human commands—all in preparation for the time the animal will be developed and strong enough to carry a rider and respond to the rider's direction. Although some breeders and trainers have in the past used force to teach young horses, most horse experts today believe that the foal's education should be kept positive and fun. Using praise and encouragement, a human trainer positively reinforces the foal's cooperation and success. For example, the trainer may lean his or her weight on the foal's back—to prepare it for the day someone will sit on its back—but only while scratching and petting the animal and only for a few seconds at a time. While speaking reassuringly, the trainer may lead the foal to walk over a pole laid on the ground and praise its success. This is the first step in it learning to jump over obstacles in the future. Talking in a happy tone of voice, the trainer may even take advantage of mud puddles to teach the foal about different surfaces. Horse trainers Tom Ainslie and Bonnie Ledbetter explain, "To demonstrate that puddles are things to walk through, you jump in. He [the foal] then experiments with a front foot and decides to take your word for it. . . . If he is a Thoroughbred, Standardbred or Quarter-horse racer, he has just taken his first lesson in moving through slop."[36]

Training for Dressage

After its general education, a young horse can be trained and conditioned for a specific sport, but when the process begins and how it continues depends upon the sport. Lipizzaner horses, for example, are bred and trained for competitive dressage. At the famous Lipica Stud Farm in Slovenia, where champion dressage Lipizzaners are bred and trained, all horses are allowed to run free for the first four years of their lives. The breeders believe that the horses are not fully mature and do not have the strength to perform difficult dressage procedures until after this age. Then the horses spend five years

TROT & GALLOP

A male foal is called a colt and a female foal is a filly. They are called colts and fillies until they are four years old.

Lipizzaners and riders perform at the Lipica Stud Farm—the birthplace of the preferred dressage breed—in Lipica, Slovenia, in 2008.

in dressage training, with one human trainer for every four horses so that the animals can learn to trust and bond with specific humans. Training begins with "straight riding," in which the horses wear bridles and saddles and learn to work on a longe line. A longe is a long strap that is snapped to the horse's bridle and held at the other end by the trainer. The horse practices circling the trainer at the center as it moves around an arena on the line and follows voice commands. Later, the horse is ridden around the arena and practices following the commands of the mounted rider. Once these skills are mastered, the horse practices balanced movements, such as lengthening and shortening its gaits on command, stepping sideways, trotting in place, and making elegant turns.

Learning dressage movements is so complex that horses spend years mastering the techniques and developing the muscles and athleticism to perform elegantly. The horses then compete at the sport for ten to fifteen years before they are permanently retired. At the best training facilities, such as the Lipica Stud Farm, training is slow and humane, and only the most skillful horses make it to top sporting events. The rest are used for non-sporting purposes such as general riding or pulling carriages. The most skillful and capable horses are identified during training, and this is true with other horses in other sporting competitions, as well. Most Thoroughbreds, for instance, do not make it to the most prestigious races either, but the best are usually identified early in their careers.

Thoroughbreds: A Different Start

Thoroughbreds begin training when they are about one year old—yearlings instead of foals. At that time, they begin a high-nutrition feeding program of high-protein feed and alfalfa hay to add weight and muscle strength. Exercising to build muscles and increase stamina usually begins with a mechanical hot walker—something like a treadmill for a person—that leads the horse around in a circle as it walks in sand at varying speeds. Like Lipizzaners, Thoroughbreds are exercised on longe lines while they practice following voice commands. Not until they are two years old are Thoroughbreds saddled and bridled. Once they are used to carrying a rider, they begin working on the training track. The horses follow a careful workout program consisting of days of running followed by days of rest and are ridden longer and faster as time passes in order to build up their stamina and speed. On the days that the horse is not galloped, it will be jogged or trotted to keep it fit but not overexercised. Young horses can be susceptible to a condition

A trainer walks a one-year-old Thoroughbred at a farm near Lexington, Kentucky. Thoroughbreds begin their race training as yearlings.

called overtraining syndrome when they are raced too much. The condition results in muscle fatigue and stress. Trainers watch their horses carefully for signs of fatigue and reduce the workout schedule if a horse begins to perform poorly.

Assuming that workout sessions go well, the horses begin galloping in timed races, and when the trainer feels they have progressed as much as they can and have become fast enough, they are trained to enter and leave a starting gate. Once that is accomplished, the best horses are ready to begin their jobs as racehorses. Throughout their careers, Thoroughbreds continue their training and workouts, usually about one hour a day, so as to remain conditioned and fit. Equally important is the careful attention paid to the horse's nutritional needs. The nonprofit Grayson-Jockey Club Research Foundation explains, "The unique racing lifestyle places high demands on equine athletes, and proper care through feeding is a crucial consideration in terms of their wellbeing and performance."[37]

Nutrition and Fitness for the Racing Team

Thoroughbreds, like all sport horses in demanding events, require high-energy feed to give them the fuel their muscles need for intense exercise. In animals, energy from food is stored in the cells as glycogen. Glycogen is the way the body stores the glucose (a kind of sugar) that is metabolized from food. Muscle stores of glycogen are burned up during training and racing, and these stores must be replaced. "For this reason," explains the Grayson-

FEEDING A CHAMPION

To help them perform at their best, adult racehorses are fed a diet composed of hay and horse feed, which can include added vitamins and supplemental fat. Young horses being trained for racing are typically fed a diet higher in crude protein and fat.

Example of Typical Race Horse Feed

Ingredients	Percent
Cracked corn	45.00
Whole oats	42.50
Soybean meal	7.50
Molasses	3.25
Calcium carbonate	0.75
Trace mineral salt	0.75
Vitamin A	varies
Vitamin E	varies

Source: P.G. Gibbs, G.D. Potter, and B.D. Scott. "Feeding Race Prospects & Racehorses in Training." Agrilife Extension, Texas A&M University. 2011.

Jockey Club Research Foundation, "many racehorses are fed large quantities of energy-rich grain, containing soluble carbohydrate or starch."[38] Carbohydrates and starch are quickly converted to glucose and easily stored as glycogen in the muscle cells. Fats, such as vegetable oils, are included in the diet, too, because muscles can use the fat for energy first, leaving some glycogen stored for use at the end of a race. Proteins, from sources such as soybeans, are fed to horses to build up and maintain body tissue. Vitamins and minerals are added to the diet, along with hay for fiber. Hay, or forage, increases the production of saliva in the horse's mouth, which helps protect its stomach lining from the acids used in digestion. The amounts of each kind of feed are individualized and based on the body weight, exercise levels, and assumed energy needs of each racehorse. In today's racing world, a Thoroughbred's nutrition is scientifically planned in order to maximize its chance to become a winning athlete.

In racing competitions, nutrition and fitness are as important for the human half of the equestrian team as they are for the horse. Western barrel racer and riding trainer Martha Josey says, "I'm very big on keeping fit. To ride your best and be competitive, you have to stay in shape. . . . I'm also into proper nutrition—lots of vegetables and fruits—and a good vitamin/mineral supplement. As a result of all I do, I almost never feel tired anymore. And I teach all of this at my clinics, too, because training your horse is only a part of it. You have to train yourself, too."[39]

Sports trainer Darrell Morgan has developed a fitness program specifically for riders in endurance events because they are so susceptible to fatigue. He says that "the physical toll taken on the rider is immense" during endurance events. Morgan emphasizes muscle strength and endurance exercises done immediately before a workout ride with the horse. He explains, "By placing the strength and conditioning workouts immediately prior to a practice ride you will fatigue your body and force it to work extra hard during the ride that follows. The harder you work your body during the pre-ride workout, the closer you will replicate the physical demands of a full endurance ride, without needing to ride

Bleeders

Bleeders are horses that bleed from their lungs during intense, galloping exercise. The condition is called EIPH (exercise-induced pulmonary hemorrhage) and is recognized by the horse getting a nosebleed after or during galloping. The horse's large lungs pump out air forcefully as it gallops, while every stride jars the horse's body. As the air rushes in and out of the lungs, it breaks the tiny blood vessels inside the lungs. The horse cannot continue its level of exercise, and its performance deteriorates. A horse may even die because the lungs can fill up with blood, and oxygen cannot get to the body. The condition is common, but no one knows exactly why, and there is no cure. Many horse experts believe the problem is hereditary, but no one has yet to find the gene or genes responsible.

EIPH can be treated with diuretics—medicines that increase urine production and reduce blood pressure. However, diuretics can cause dehydration if they are not carefully administered. For this reason, and because diuretics can cause rapid weight loss, their use in racing is outlawed in Europe, Australia, Japan, and Hong Kong. In the United States, diuretic treatment is legal, but controversial.

anywhere near as long." Morgan also helps endurance riders plan for their nutritional needs during the endurance event itself. He recommends "bulking up"[40] on carbohydrates during rest stops because carbohydrates are metabolized quickly for energy. Since fats and proteins are absorbed slowly, he tells riders to avoid them during the race, but to eat these foods in extra quantities in the two days after the race in order to physically recover from the fatigue.

Nutrition Problems in the Racing World

Jockeys in Thoroughbred racing may face the most grueling conditioning problems of all equestrian athletes. Retired

TROT & GALLOP

Although sport horses are fit and trim athletes, researchers in England say that horses used for leisure or kept as companion animals have obesity rates similar to humans, with about 50 percent of these horses either overweight or obese.

professional jockey Frank Lovato Jr. says, "It is said that pound for pound, jockeys are the fittest athletes in the world."[41] Jockeys have to maintain the strength and flexibility to ride and control their spirited horses, but at the same time, they are required to keep a low body weight. Lovato says that the ideal weight for a jockey is about 110 pounds (49.9kg). Staying so lightweight while remaining healthy and strong is not easy, and most jockeys struggle to control their weight. Jockeys' Guild, the organization of professional jockeys, reports that many jockeys eat poorly in order to maintain racing weights. Jockeys often skip meals, limit drinking fluids, eat and then make themselves vomit afterwards (purging), or take laxatives or diet pills. The Jockeys' Guild says, "These actions can be dangerous for the jockeys, leading to dehydration, loss of concentration, and decrease in mental and physical abilities."[42]

Many jockeys feel they have no choice except to ignore their nutritional needs. Jockey John Velazquez, for instance, controls his weight by starving himself throughout the day and then eating one meal in the evening. Typically, he eats a half cup of dry cereal in the morning and then sips a bit of coffee, sucks juice from an orange, and takes a single bite of banana off and on throughout the day. He drinks water only before his evening meal. Velazquez says, "Is it normal? No, it's not normal. It's part of my life. It comes with the territory."[43]

The Jockeys' Guild is trying to change the weight demands for jockeys by persuading racetracks around the United States to agree to a standard and increased minimum weight limit for jockeys. The organization also supports research to study the long-term effects of poor nutrition and eating disorders on professional jockeys. In cooperation with the guild, researchers are trying to develop healthy nutritional guidelines for jockeys. At the University of Delaware, researchers O. Sue Snider and Nancy Cotugna developed a nutritional program that emphasizes eating small snacks

Jockey John Bisono is weighed at the Pimlico Race Course in Baltimore, Maryland, after winning a 2013 race. Jockeys must be strong and agile but also must keep their weight low— two objectives that sometimes conflict.

of low-calorie, nutritious foods throughout the day. In a 2012 study of ninety-nine British jockeys, however, researcher Nóra Ní Fhlannagáin discovered that 82 percent of the jockeys practice dangerous weight-loss methods, even when they have been given dietary advice. Ní Fhlannagáin says that this may "indicate that there is resistance to dietitians and sports nutritionists in horse racing as jockeys feel that their advice is unrealistic, difficult to follow or unlikely to bring them down to riding weight."[44]

Dedicated to the Sport They Love

Almost all jockeys suffer to maintain weight and fitness, but they are dedicated to racing, despite the problems. Jockey Willie Martinez explains, "A lot of people don't know the sacrifices we make in this business, the things we put ourselves through. But we choose to do this because we love it. . . ."[45] A love of horses and racing may be what ultimately makes a winning horse-and-rider team. Jockeys, as well as owners and trainers, often say that dedication to their sport, as well as understanding and relating to their horses, can be as important as fitness for success in equestrian sport.

CHAPTER 7

Psychology and the Human/Horse Interaction

Unlike the nonliving components in other sports, a horse is not a machine or a piece of sporting equipment. It is a living, breathing creature with individuality, intelligence, feelings, and a language all its own. The fittest, best-fed, most highly trained horse may not perform at its best without a human handler who understands and cares about the horse's psychology. Riders who are aware of and are sensitive to the nature of their mounts are often the best equestrians. They are the athletes who are able to form a real relationship with their horses and optimize the horse/human interaction.

The Mind of a Prey Animal

Perhaps the most important thing to understand about the horse is that it is a prey animal. Prey animals are vegetarians that are hunted and eaten by predators. Prey animals are always on the alert for danger and have to maintain a constant vigilance for any threats to their lives. All prey animals have some sort of strategy for surviving and avoiding becoming a meal for a predator. For horses, the major survival strategy is the instinct (an inborn pattern of behavior) for flight when danger seems to threaten. This innate drive to flee in the face of danger overrules all other instincts from the time

the horse is born, including the instinct to eat or drink, to mate, to socialize, or to fight in the face of danger. American quarter horse trainer Lindsay Grice explains, "Prey animals need to be more perceptive than predators in order to survive. When they perceive frightening stimuli, they flee and don't stop to ask questions."[46] A horse's wide field of vision (with eyes on each side of its head instead of forward-facing) and acute hearing make it quick to detect sights and sounds that humans (who are predators) may not even notice, and rather than question whether the detected stimulus is truly threatening, its flight instinct urges it to escape.

The psychology of a horse as a prey animal has a direct effect on its interaction with people and how it can be trained. The horse's tendency to fear new things and to try to flee from danger explains why young horses have to be taught not to fear things like mud puddles and starting gates. It also explains why the best horse trainers take a slow and easy approach to gaining the horse's trust. As an example, prey animals do not walk in a straight line; they

The alpha male of a herd, who is responsible for safety, stands guard against a human intruder giving the rest of the group an opportunity to flee.

edge around things, retreat from unfamiliar objects, and approach any new situation cautiously. Predators do walk in straight lines; they walk right up to or stalk their prey and then attack by running down the prey. Humans who walk right up to horses or the things that horses fear are acting like predators and are losing their horses' trust. As trainer Emily Johnson points out, "How can a prey animal trust actions that speak of a predatory nature?"[47] People who learn to behave like horses instead of like predators are the ones who have the best relationships with and get the best performances from their horses.

Member of the Social Herd

Fortunately for the human/horse interaction, horses are born with a gregarious, social instinct that makes them want to be part of a herd. For horses, the herd (other horses) represents normalcy and comfort. Prey animals like horses group together because there is safety in numbers. In the herd, the leader—or alpha animal—is responsible for the herd's safety and provides each of the other horses with a feeling of security. In a horse herd, the lead mare directs the movements of the others and guides them to flee when dangers threaten. This is the relationship that every horse needs. Trainer Julie Goodnight explains, "One of the most fundamental concepts in understanding horses is that beyond all else in life, what a horse wants is safety and comfort. They do not want to fear for their lives; they want to feel safe, comfortable and taken care of, so they can relax and not have to think too hard or make any decisions. In short, what the horse wants most is a benevolent leader that will provide him with security and comfort."[48] If the human half of the human/horse partnership can become the leader in their herd of two, he or she will gain the horse's trust and cooperation in any equestrian endeavor.

The benevolent leader is dominant but caring, inspiring trust and confidence. Horse leaders use horse language to command respect and to make the herd feel comfortable and relaxed. Human leaders, by behaving like horse leaders and learning horse language, can accomplish the same goals.

Reading Body Language

Horse language is mainly body language, and horses use their whole bodies to communicate. For example, a horse's ears are generally pointed forward if it is relaxed, but if the ears are pointed sharply forward and the nostrils are flared while the eyes are wide and the head and neck are raised high, the horse is alert, frightened, and ready to flee. When the tail is pressed against the rear, a horse is signaling fear,

The Horse Whisperer

Buck Brannaman is a horse trainer who has often been called a horse whisperer because of the way he can understand and psychologically heal traumatized and troubled horses. Nicholas Evans, the author who wrote the best-selling book *The Horse Whisperer* (which was also made into a movie), says that the inspiration for his book was Brannaman. A horse whisperer is someone who trains a horse with gentle methods that consider the mind, needs, and psychology of the horse. Other trainers have been called horse whisperers, but Brannaman is one of the most famous, admired, and respected. Brannaman says he loves horses because they saved his life. He was born in 1962 and grew up around horses in the western United States. He says they were his only friends. His father was so abusive and cruel that the boy was removed and sent to a foster home when he was twelve. Living a childhood of fear made Brannaman sensitive to fear in others. He says today, "There's only one thing I owe my dad: that I can understand how an animal feels when it's scared for its life." So, even though he is the leader with horses, Brannaman uses gentleness and sensitivity to help them become trusting, affectionate, and happy.

Quoted in Christopher Middleton. "The Horse Whisperer: 'My Dad Taught Me to Understand Fear.'" *Telegraph*, April 17, 2012. www.telegraph.co.uk/culture /tvandradio/9206938/The-horse-whisperer-My-dad-taught-me-to-understand -fear.html.

too. The alert horse carries its tail high, while a fiercely swishing tail can signal anger or frustration.

A good human leader reads the horse's body language and solves any problem when necessary. Tom Ainslie and Bonnie Ledbetter tell a story of one such situation. A student at a school for animal studies saw a stallion in a stall at the school showing great signs of fear. The horse's eyes were wide, and it was sweating. It had refused to eat or sleep and remained frozen in the back of its stall. The horse handlers in the barn had not read the body language correctly and thought the horse was sick. The student had previously worked with the stallion, so she patiently approached the situation, talking soothingly and stroking the horse until she was able to clip a rope to its halter and lead it out of the stall. The stallion followed the trusted student and then turned back toward the bales of hay stacked beside the horse's stall entrance. Its ears and nose were pointed sharply toward the hay bales. At the student's suggestion, the barn workers moved the bales of hay and discovered a large snake hiding underneath them.

After the snake was killed, the student allowed the stallion to approach the dead body, and his whole attitude changed. He became confident and assertive. His head came up, his ears pricked high, and he reared and stomped the body to bits. With that task finished, the horse assumed a relaxed posture and calmly returned to its stall. Ainslie and Ledbetter say that this story illustrates the principles that a good human leader follows. The principles include: "Recognition that a problem exists [by reading the body language].... Identifying the general nature of the problem [fear].... Treating the problem in the context of a sound working relationship [the horse trusted the student]."[49]

Flared nostrils and ears pointed sharply forward usually mean the horse is frightened.

Understanding Horse Emotions Through Body Language

Horses experience and display many emotions with their bodies. A curious horse, for example, points its nose, eyes, and ears directly toward the new object that it wants to investigate. As a prey animal, it does not walk directly to the object, but spends a lot of time circling it, backing off for a while, and then moving closer. Finally, when assured that the object is not a threat, it cranes its neck forward, touches it with its muzzle, and sniffs thoroughly. Trainers and jockeys sometimes see signs of this behavior when they bring a horse to a new racing track. The horse stands still, looks all around with its head and neck up, sniffs the air, and listens for any new sounds with ears forward. When the handler understands and accepts these actions with patience, the horse not only trusts more, but also ends up being a more confident and eager animal.

Eager horses display a particular body language, too. An eager show jumping horse, for instance, stamps its foot in impatience to get started, shakes its head, and dances sideways. It turns its ears back to hear the signals of the rider or pricks them forward toward the first jump. The horse signals its happiness with a raised tail and prancing. When particularly happy, it may drop its head and then flip it upward and make a circle in the air with its nose. Ainslie and Ledbetter say, "A race or show horse that approaches competition strutting with a raised tail is happy about the whole thing, including the noise of the crowd."[50]

Seabiscuit: The Emotions for Success

The human leader can make all the difference in a horse's performance, because he or she plays such a large role in determining whether the horse is happy and eager or sour

TROT & GALLOP

When a horse wants to signal submission to a dominant leader, it opens and closes its mouth in a chewing motion that imitates a nursing foal's mouth movements with its mother.

and angry. The legendary Thoroughbred Seabiscuit is a famous example of a horse that became a winner because someone read his body language and cared about his emotions. Seabiscuit had an excellent genetic heritage; he was the grandson of Man o' War, who was named the racehorse of the century in the early 1900s. Seabiscuit, however, was small for a Thoroughbred, and by the time he was three years old, in 1936, he was angry, uncooperative, lazy, and losing races. As a two-year-old, Seabiscuit, although still immature, had been forced to race thirty-five times. He was trained forcefully and often whipped when he raced. He was exhausted and trusted no one. Then trainer Tom Smith persuaded his boss at their racing stable to buy the horse. Smith was called a horse whisperer by people who knew him, and he used his understanding of horse language and psychology to change Seabiscuit's life.

An angry horse makes its emotions clear. It may turn its back on the handler who enters its stall. Its body is tense; it tenses or flattens its ears; its upper lip quivers and curls; it slaps its tail against its rear. It never cooperates with its handler completely and responds slowly to commands, acting as if it has no energy. An exhausted horse is also uncooperative. Its body looks droopy, and the horse often dozes standing up. Seabiscuit demonstrated all of these behaviors, and Smith understood their meaning. Smith worked to gain the horse's trust by being a kind and patient leader. Because the horse was underweight, he fed Seabiscuit a high-nutrition diet, and he allowed the horse to sleep as much as it wanted. He rode the horse, but not on a track, and allowed Seabiscuit to run away with him; he made no attempt to guide the horse and let Seabiscuit do what he wanted. Recognizing the needs of a herd animal, Smith also provided Seabiscuit with friends. He stabled Seabiscuit with a calm, old pony named Pumpkin, a stray dog, and a spider monkey. All three slept with the horse every night. And Seabiscuit gradually relaxed and stopped feeling angry and suspicious.

With trust and renewed energy, Seabiscuit began a training program on the exercise track with a jockey who never whipped the horse, who appreciated the horse's renewed spirit, and who fed Seabiscuit sugar cubes. Seabiscuit be-

Tom Smith, the horse trainer who first saw potential in Seabiscuit, leads him into a race at Belmont Park in New York.

came a winning racehorse. He was impressively fast, competitively spirited, and a champion. People wondered what miracles Smith had worked to turn a lazy, angry horse into an eager, happy horse. Smith, however, knew that no miracles were involved. He once explained, "It's easy to talk to horses if you understand his language. Horses stay the same from the day they are born until the day they die, they are only changed by the way people treat them."[51]

Motivation: Can a Horse Have the Will to Win?

Laura Hillenbrand, who authored the famous book *Seabiscuit: An American Legend*, wrote of the horse after he was trained by Smith, "The fire that had kept Seabiscuit frustrated and unruly now fueled a bounding will to win."[52] Some experts question whether racehorses really have a "will to win." They emphasize that a horse just wants to feel comfortable and acquiesces to a handler's commands because it has learned—through repetition and reinforcement—to avoid pressure and to feel comfortable by doing what it has been taught. Horses understand pressure applied to their bodies. An alpha horse, for example, uses body pressure to push another horse away from a source of food or a comfortable, shady spot. The submissive horse moves away, thereby eliminating the pressure and moving from a condition of discomfort to one of comfort. Trainers say this is why horses respond to the pressure of reins, bits, whips, or the rider's legs. By moving away from the pressure, they are following commands (such as turning left or moving forward). According to this theory, the horse is merely interested in pleasing itself, and the best way to do that is to cooperate with the commands it has learned.

Other experts suggest that the will to win is really a physiological reaction of the brain, determined by genetic heritage. According to this idea, some horses are simply better equipped to perform because of an innate difference in their brains. In all living things, muscle cells use oxygen extracted from the blood for the energy to keep running or exercising. At some point, the maximum amount of uptake of oxygen is reached, and the animal cannot continue. It is exhausted and must slow down or stop. The decision that the exercise can go no further, theorizes Timothy D. Noakes, is made in the brain. He calls this idea the "central governor theory."[53] The central governor in the brain, he says, senses the level of physical effort and slows it down before complete exhaustion can occur. A scientific article from the company Performance Genetics LLC summarizes, "In Dr. Noakes's 'central governor' theory, the decision to slow down or stop during exercise isn't the result of an absolute physical limit. Instead, the brain applies the brakes proactively to prevent the horse from reaching these limits. After all, if a horse really did run to the absolute edge of its physical limits, it would be dead."[54] This theory sug-

TROT & GALLOP

A horse's brain weighs 1.5 to 2 pounds (0.7 to 0.9kg), about the size of a human child's, while an adult human brain weighs about 3 pounds (1.4kg). Much of the human brain is devoted to language and fine motor skills, but much of the horse's brain is devoted to perceiving and analyzing information from the environment.

Clever Hans

Clever Hans was a horse known as a genius throughout Europe during the 1890s. His owner, William von Osten of Germany, had taught the horse some amazing feats. Von Osten could ask the horse to add or subtract numbers, and Clever Hans would stamp his foot until he got to the right answer. He could also tell time and tap out the days of the week (one tap for Monday, two for Tuesday, and so on). Von Osten and the general public were convinced that the horse was brilliant. The explanation for the genius horse, however, lay in body language—von Osten's body language. Clever Hans, like all horses, could read the body language of his owner. Without realizing it, von Osten tensed his body, leaned forward slightly, or got an expectant look on his face when Clever Hans reached the correct answer. These subtle body movements were the signal to the horse to stop. The horse was always rewarded for the correct answers, so he carefully observed and performed as von Osten wished. Although all horses may not be as clever as Clever Hans, they all have the ability to read their owners' body language and learn to respond to the cues.

gests that what appears to be a will to win is only the existence of a sort of central governor that does not "put on the brakes" as soon in one horse as it does in other horses.

Bonded and Loving to Win

Despite scientific theories to the contrary, many equestrian athletes believe that some horses do have a real will to win. Penny Chenery, the owner of Secretariat, the great racehorse of the 1970s, believed the animal understood about winning and losing. She once said, "I do think we humanize the animals we love. But Secretariat was like that. After he got beat, he wouldn't come to the webbing (the barrier across the stall door). He wouldn't be consoled, saying, in

Penny Chenery leads Secretariat and jockey Ron Turcotte to the Winner's Circle at Belmont Park racetrack in Elmont, New York, after winning the 1973 Marlboro Cup. Earlier that year, Secretariat had won the Triple Crown: the Kentucky Derby, the Preakness Stakes, and the Belmont Stakes.

effect, I know I messed up." Chenery believed Secretariat was smart and wanted to win. She added, "We don't have any dumb champions. They have to want to run. You can't force them into being dedicated to running. The horse has to 'get it.'"[55] According to everyone who worked with him, Secretariat "got it" and never needed to be pushed to race. The horse was happy, eager, and bonded to all the people who cared for him, and the riders, trainers, handlers, and his owner loved the big horse in return. In the end, whether scientific or not, perhaps the most important factor for success in any equestrian sport is the intangible, immeasurable relationship between horse and human and the care and affection they feel for one another.

NOTES

Chapter 1: An Overview of Equestrian Competitive Sports

1. Dr. William J. Jordan. "Domestication Versus Taming." Circus Watch WA. http://circuswatchwa.org/domestication.htm.
2. Quoted in Emily Sohn. "Humans Tamed Horses All Over the World." *Discovery News*, January 30, 2012. http://news.discovery.com/animals/horses-domesticated-120130.html.
3. Quoted in "So You Want to Learn How to Play Polo?" Horsetalk.co.nz. www.horsetalk.co.nz/saferide/learn-polo.shtml.
4. Judith Draper, Debby Sly, and Sarah Muir. *The Ultimate Book of the Horse and Rider*. London: Hermes House, Anness Publishing Ltd., 2005, p. 377.
5. Heather Toms. "Horses Ideal for Show Jumping." HorsesHorses.net, April 10, 2012. http://horsehorses.net/horse-training-techniques/horses-ideal-for-show-jumping.html.

Chapter 2: The Physics of Equestrian Sports

6. Quoted in "Newton's Laws of Mo-

tion." Glen Research Center: National Aeronautics and Space Administration (NASA). www.grc.nasa.gov/WWW/k-12/airplane/newton.html.
7. Ibid.
8. Quoted in Starr Crusenberry. "Pimlico Starting Gate Crew." *Baltimore Stories: Tales from Charm City*. www.baltimorestories.com/main.cfm?nid=9&tid=145.
9. Quoted in "Newton's Laws of Motion."
10. Donald Simanek. "The Horse and Cart Problem." Donald Simanek's Pages, Lock Haven University of Pennsylvania. www.lhup.edu/~dsimanek/physics/horsecart.htm.
11. Quoted in Pat Murphy. "The Woman Who Flies Through the Air." *Santa Ynez Valley Journal*, April 14, 2011. www.syvjournal.com/archive/9/15/8204.

Chapter 3: Biomechanics and the Horse and Rider

12. Steven Vogel. *Cats' Paws and Catapults*. New York: W.W. Norton, 1998, p. 9.
13. Hilary M. Clayton. *The Dynamic Horse: A Biomechanical Guide to*

Equine Movement and Performance. Mason, MI: Sport Horse Publications, 2004, p. 12.

14. Clayton. The Dynamic Horse, p 12.
15. Gideon Ariel. "The Horse Racing Connection." From *The Discus Thrower and His Dream Factory,* chapter 15, p. 5. www.arielnet.com /chapters/show/gba-wri-01002-15 /the-race-horsesconnection.
16. Ariel. "The Horse Racing Connection," p. 10.
17. Christine Woodford. "Equine Biomechanics and Gait Analysis," p. 42. www.vipsvet.net/articles/biome chanics.pdf.
18. Sheila Schils, "Biomechanics of Jumping." Equinew.com. www.equi new.com/jumping.htm.
19. Sheila Schils, "Biomechanics of Jumping."
20. Sian E.M. Lawson. "Pushing Off the Ground—Newton and Take Off" and "Be Your Own Biomechanist: What to Look For in Your Photos." *Equine Mechanics,* May 24, 2012. http://equinemechanics.co.uk/page /2.
21. Quoted in Jeffrey Kluger. "Secrets of Jockeying: Why Horses Go Fast." *Time,* July 21, 2009. www.time .com/time/health/article/0,8599 ,1911101,00.html.

Chapter 4: The Environmental Factors of Equestrian Sports

22. Chrisann Ware. "Saddle Fit as it Affects the Equine Biomechanics."
Equethy. www.equethy.com/page5 .htm.
23. Ware. "Saddle Fit as it Affects the Equine Biomechanics."
24. Ware. "Saddle Fit as it Affects the Equine Biomechanics."
25. Quoted in Fiona Carruthers. "Cruel Twist to the Elite Sport of Dressage." *Financial Review,* July 27, 2012. www.afr.com/p/lifestyle/sport /olympics/cruel_twist_to_the_ elite_sport_of_rb4kg1oAnuBH6u HYeRwjZI.
26. Quoted in "Horse Racing: The Pack is Secret to Success." Discovery News, March 7, 2012. http://news .discovery.com/animals/horse-ra cing-scientists-secret-success-pack draft-120307.html.
27. Quoted in Teresa Pitman. "Horses Heat Up to 10 Times Faster Than People—Study." Horsetalk.co.nz, June 29, 2010. www.horsetalk.co .nz/news/2010/06/159.shtml.

Chapter 5: The Right Horse for the Sport

28. "Applications of Genome Study— Simple Hereditary Diseases." Horse Genome Project, 2011. www.uky.edu/Ag/Horsemap/hgp diseases.html.
29. "Frequently Asked Questions: Why Are There So Many Colors of Horses?" Horse Genome Project, 2011. www.uky.edu/Ag/Horsemap /hgpfaq4.html.
30. Glynis Giddings. "Horse Conformation." Horse Genetics. www.horse

-genetics.com/horse-conforma
tion.html.

31. Quoted in "Genetic Test for 'Speed
Gene' in Thoroughbred Horses."
ScienceDaily, February 3, 2010.
www.sciencedaily.com/releases/20
10/02/100202144204.htm.

32. Quoted in "Jockeying for Genetic Advantage: DNA Analysis to
Evaluate Thoroughbreds." *Science-
Daily*, May 2, 2012. www.science
daily.com/releases/2012/05/12050
2162520.htm.

33. Quoted in "Jockeying for Genetic
Advantage: DNA Analysis to Evaluate Thoroughbreds."

34. Ben Baugh. "Alpha's Heart Played
Huge Role in Capturing Horse-of-
the-Year Honors." *Aiken Standard*,
November 27, 2012. www.aiken
standard.com/article/20121127
/AIK0101/121129607.

Chapter 6: Training, Conditioning, and Nutrition

35. Robert N. Oglesby. "Imprinting the
Newborn Foal." HorseTalk.co.nz.
www.horsetalk.co.nz/breeding/tha
-imprint.shtml#axzz2d3OWHyMb.

36. Tom Ainslie and Bonnie Ledbetter.
The Body Language of Horses. New
York: William Morrow, 1980, p. 145.

37. Grayson-Jockey Club Research
Foundation. "Horsemen's Update:
Managing the Thoroughbred Diet."
Welfare and Safety of the Race-
horse Summit, January 2008, p. 1.
www.grayson-jockeyclub.org/news

38. Grayson-Jockey Club Research
Foundation. "Horsemen's Update:
Managing the Thoroughbred
Diet," p. 1.

39. Quoted in Steve Archer. "Fitness Secrets of the Stars." Equisearch. www
.equisearch.com/horses_riding
_training/western/eqstars697.

40. Darrell Morgan. "Endurance Horse
Riding: Strength, Conditioning
and Nutrition." Building Better
Bodies. http://ibuildbetterbodies
.com/general/endurance-horse-ri
ding-strength-conditioning-and
-nutrition.

41. Frank Lovato Jr. "What It Takes
to Be a Jockey." *Barn Mice*, August 2008. http://barnmice.com
/profiles/blogs/what-it-takes-to
-be-jockey-by.

42. UD Helps Keep Jockeys Race
Ready," Nutritional Section, Jockeys' Guild, August 30, 2010. www
.jockeysguild.com/nutritional
section.html.

43. Quoted in Richard Rosenblatt.
"Jockeys are Still Battling Weight
Issues." Associated Press, April 29,
2008, reprinted at Jockeys' Guild:
Nutritional Section. www.jockeys
guild.com/nutritionalsection.html.

44. Quoted in "British Jockeys Persist
with Risky Weight-Loss Methods."
Horsetalk.co.nz, March 1, 2012.
www.horsetalk.co.nz/news/2012
/03/012.shtml.

45. Quoted in Jennie Rees. "Now a
Breeders' Cup Winner, Jockey Willie Martinez Keeps Rooted at Tampa

Bay Downs." *Courier-Journal.com*, December 7, 2012. http://blogs.courier-journal.com/racing/2012/12/07/now-a-breeders-cup-winner-jockey-willie-martinez-keeps-rooted-at-tampa-bay-downs.

Chapter 7: Psychology and the Human/Horse Interaction

46. Lindsay Grice. "Thinking Like a Horse Simplifies Training." Ontario Ministry of Agriculture and Food, October 2006. www.omafra.gov.on.ca/english/livestock/horses/facts/06-097.htm.
47. Emily Johnson. "Horse Behavior and Psychology (Part I)." Mountain Rose Horsemanship Training. http://mountainrosehorsemanship.com/resources/leadline02.php.
48. Julie Goodnight. "Horse Psychology & the Language of Horses." University of Florida, 2007. http://cflag.ifas.ufl.edu/documents/2007EquineInstit/HorsePsychLanguage.pdf.
49. Ainslie and Ledbetter, *The Body Language of Horses*, p. 103.
50. Ainslie and Ledbetter, *The Body Language of Horses*, p. 68.
51. Quoted in Kyle Williams. "His Horses Spoke for Him." Washington Racing Hall of Fame, *Washington Thoroughbred*, August 2004, p. 658. www.washingtonthoroughbred.com/WaTbStats/HOF_Smith.htm.
52. Laura Hillenbrand. *Seabiscuit: An American Legend.* New York: Ballantine, 2003, p. 129.
53. Timothy D. Noakes. "The Central Governor Model in 2012: Eight New Papers Deepen Our Understanding of the Regulation of Human Exercise Performance." *British Journal of Sports Medicine*, vol. 46, iss. 1, January 2012, p. 1. http://bjsm.bmj.com/content/46/1/1.full.
54. "The Will to Win." Performance Genetics, February 22, 2012. http://performancegenetics.com/2012/02/22/the-will-to-win.
55. Quoted in Bill Doolittle. "Secretariat: Super Genius." Secretariat.com. www.secretariat.com/fan-club/writers-forum/secretariat-super-genius.

GLOSSARY

acceleration: The rate at which an object changes its velocity.

air resistance: The force that resists or pushes back on an object as it moves through the air. Also called drag.

allele: One of two or more variations or alternative forms of a gene.

center of gravity: The point in a body where its total weight and mass are in perfect balance.

chromosome: A long string of a group of genes that carry hereditary information.

conformation: The physical structure of a horse's body.

dehydration: The loss of the water and salts necessary for normal body function.

deoxyribonucleic acid (DNA): The genetic material in cells that codes for body structure and functioning. DNA is arranged as a long, double-stranded molecule called a double helix.

energy: The ability to perform work; the power that can create motion, overcome resistance, or cause a physical change in the body.

gene: A segment of DNA on a chromosome that carries specific hereditary information.

gravity: The force of attraction or pull between any two physical bodies that have mass.

imprinting: A rapid learning process in which a newborn animal develops recognition and bonds to its mother or a mother substitute.

inertia: The tendency for an object at rest to remain at rest or an object in motion to remain in motion unless acted on by an outside force.

instinct: An inborn fixed pattern of behavior that does not have to be learned.

momentum: Mass in motion; any moving object has this quantity, which is defined in physics as mass multiplied by velocity.

mutation: A change in the DNA coding that is permanent and can be passed on to future generations.

selective breeding: The process of intentionally mating animals to achieve particular genetic traits in the offspring.

stimulus: Any object or event in the environment that is perceived by the senses and causes a response or reaction in any living thing.

tack: Any equipment used to ride horses, such as saddles, harnesses, bits, and bridles.

temperament: An animal's nature—its mental and emotional traits.

trait: A physical or behavioral characteristic that is determined by genes and/or influenced by the environment.

velocity: The rate at which an object changes its position.

Books

Jane Kidd. *To Be a Dressage Rider*. North Pomfret, VT: The Pony Club/Half Halt, 2006. The author explains dressage techniques and training both for horses and young riders who want to begin competing in the sport of dressage.

Dandi Daley Mackall, *You and Your Horse: How to Whisper Your Way into Your Horse's Life*. New York: Aladdin Paperbacks, 2009. In this book, readers can learn about a horse's psychology, its senses, and its communications. The book's goal is to help human handlers form strong relationships and friendships with their horses by understanding their needs.

Deborah A. Parks, *Nature's Machines: The Story of Biomechanist Mimi Koehl*. Washington, D.C.: Joseph Henry, 2006. This book explains the biomechanics of living things and the way the science has developed by examining the life of scientist Mimi Koehl, who has spent her career studying the physics and engineering of nature.

Lesley Ward, *Jumping for Kids*. North Adams, MA: Storey, 2007. This book is designed to help young, beginning equestrians learn to jump on a horse and to teach their horses to jump. It includes chapters on building fences, training exercises, show jumping, and cross-country events that include jumping obstacles, as well as riding and balancing advice for the young rider.

John Woodward, *Horses: The Ultimate Treasury*. New York: DK Children, 2012. From wild horses and domestication to breeds of horses to working and show horses to horses in fiction, this book covers the world of horses from many angles. It includes a description of the famous Spanish Riding School and its dressage horses.

Websites

HorseBreedsList (www.horsebreedslist .com). Visitors to this large site can click on different breeds of horses to learn about the history and character of each breed.

Horse Genetics (www.horse-genetics .com). At this very extensive website, visitors can learn about the basics of horse genetics, as well as specific information about breeds, horse colors and patterns, breeding, and the latest genetic research. The site includes numerous photographs of different breeds of horses.

The Jockey (www.thejockey.com). This site was developed by a retired jockey to educate people about jockeys and their careers. Many video clips of Thoroughbred races are available for viewers.

Physics4Kids (www.physics4kids.com /index.html). This site is not just for kids but for anyone who wants to learn about physics. The section on motion explores Newton's laws of motion and important concepts such as acceleration, velocity, gravity, and speed.

Secretariat.com (www.secretariat.com). This site is devoted to the historic racehorse and includes detailed descriptions of his racing history, his legacy, and the humans in his life. Many historic photographs are included.

INDEX

Skeleton
    locomotion/gait relation, 35–36
    studies, 10
Skijoring, 58, *58*
Skill requirements
    competitive horse racing, 16
    dressage, 16–17
    endurance riding, 18
    polo, 15, 16
    Western riding events, 15–16
Social instincts of horses, 90
Standardbred horses, 64, 66, 79
Survival strategies for wild horses, 88–90

T

Thoroughbred horses
    anatomy and physiology, *40*
    biomechanical competitive edge, 41–42
    breeders, *77*
    genetic inheritance and, 71–74, *73*
    historical background, 12

jockey riding styles, 47
nutrition program, 81, 83–85
training procedures, *77*, 81–82, *82*
Training
    dressage, 12, 16–17, 79–81, *80*
    first lessons, 76–79
    human/horse interaction, 88–98
    imprint training, 76–77
    nutrition and fitness, 83–87
    Thoroughbreds, *77*, 81–82, *82*
Turkey, horse-based games, 12

W

Western riding events, 15, 38, 64, 66, 84
Western saddles, 50–51
Westphalian horses, 66
White Turf race (Switzerland), *58*
Will to win, 74–75, 95–98
Work types, for horses, 14*t*
World Equestrian Games, *19*

PICTURE CREDITS

Cover images: © Anastasjia Popova/ Shutterstock.com; © holbox/Shutter stock.com; © Mikhail Pogosov/ Shutterstock.com

© Adrian Dennis/AFP/Getty Images, 42

© Andy Cross/The Denver Post via Getty Images, 77

© AP Images, 98

© AP Images/James Crisp, 82

© Bill Boch/Botanica/Getty Images, 51

© Bob Thomas/Getty Images, 34

© Charles Bertram/Lexington Herald-Leader/MCT via Getty Images, 19

© Chris Jackson/Getty Images, 80

© Christof Koepsel/Bongarts/Getty Images, 52

© David Robertson/Getty Images, 56

© Eadweard Muybridge/Time Life Pictures/Getty Images, 36

© Eric Lafforgue/Gamma-Rapho via Getty Images, 9

© Gale, Cengage Learning, 14, 26, 31, 40, 44, 55, 67, 83

© Hope Ryden/National Geographic Creative/Getty Images, 89

© Jamie Squire/Getty Images, 38

© Jeanne White/Science Source/Getty Images, 65

© John MacDougall/AFP/Getty Images, 17

© Juan Mabromata/AFP/Getty Images, 70

© Karin Sahib/AFP/Getty Images, 63

© Mark Dadswell/Getty Images, 24, 25, 28

© Martin Castellan/Alamy, 49

© Matthew Stockman/Getty Images, 46

© NY Daily News Archive via Getty Images, 95

© Patrick Smith/Getty Images, 54, 87

© Paul Hodgson/Alamy, 92

© Scott Barbour/Getty Images, 58

© Tim Webb/Lexington Herald-Leader/MCT via Getty Images, 73

© Universal History Archive/Getty Images, 11

© Vince Caligiuri/Getty Images, 32

Toney Allman holds a BS from Ohio State University and an MA from the University of Hawaii. She currently lives in Virginia and has written more than thirty nonfiction books for students on a variety of scientific topics.